City Dog Walking
Safety & Etiquette

Sunny Weber

City Dog Walking
Safety & Etiquette

SUNNY WEBER

PUPS & PURRS
PRESS

City Dog Walking Safety & Etiquette
Published by Pups and Purrs Press
Denver, CO

Library of Congress Control Number: 2018946417
ISBN: 978-0-9966612-5-6
PETS / Dogs / Training

Cover design by NZ Graphics
Photography by Patty's Pet Photography

QUANTITY PURCHASES: Schools, non-profits, animal
rescues, shelters, sanctuaries, and other organizations may
qualify for special terms when ordering quantities of this title.
For information, email
Sunny@SunnyWeber.com.

PUPS & PURRS
P R E S S

DENVER, CO

For Jessie, Bailey & Brillo
who lovingly made me a foster-flunky.

CONTENTS

INTRODUCTION

Why read a book on a "simple" activity such as dog walking? All you need is a dog, a leash, and a collar right? Theoretically, yes. But to fully engage yourself and your dog in public, there are many factors that will need to be addressed. Some factors will be obvious, such as how to keep yourself and your dog safe. Some factors will be subtle, such as the need for socially accepted manners in interactions with others on your route. Some factors will be complete surprises, such as walking route dangers, hazards, and encounters.

I have been a daily dog walker for almost thirty years. I have never found a comprehensive guide for all the situations I have found myself in with my dogs. City (urban) and neighborhood (suburban) walking is rife with complications that present confusing scenarios for all dog owners. Our duties as sensitive pet guardians encompass (1) making sure our dogs are safe; (2) ensuring a fun, positive and pleasant form of physical and mental exercise for them; and (3) making sure our dogs' behaviors (and our own) are socially responsible. Walking dogs in environments meant for human habitation means that our dogs are forced into unnatural environments for their species. Dog walking is not "easy" every day, or in every scenario. This book is a culmination of experiences I have had—and learned from—in which I felt uneasy, unsafe, or unknowledgeable. Because my dog families have encompassed a wide variety of breeds, ages, sizes, weights, and intelligence levels, I gathered what I believe is a comprehensive package of advice for dog walkers who truly wish to provide their canine exercise buddies with the most rewarding, deeply bonding and enjoyable experiences.

In this book I will cover the history of dog-human companionship, the development of shared living environments and lifestyles, what dogs need in those lifestyles, dog-human partnership philosophy, equipment needed for safe and enjoyable walking together, dog-human communication, community manners, and dog-human safety. I will discuss encounters with automobile traffic, environmental hazards, bicyclists, skateboarders, runners, wildlife, and other dogs (on-leash, off-leash, stray, shy, aggressive, friendly).

I hope that this information will help you provide your vulnerable dog with the protection, enjoyment, companionship, and advocacy every dog deserves. My goal is to help you see the human world through your dog's eyes so that you will be prepared to plan for your dog's needs.

Although many people love their dogs as their children, they must see the world as their dog does—which in many cases is not that different from the way a toddler sees. Trusting, naïve, vulnerable and focused on you, your dog will need you to see before she sees, and need you to understand how she mentally and emotionally processes novel stimuli. You must also be prepared to advocate for your dog and protect her.

I hope this information helps you become the benevolent leader your dog deserves. She trusts you with her life and addressing her needs should be your top priority.

CHAPTER 1

THE HISTORY OF THE
DOG-HUMAN PARTNERSHIP

PREHISTORIC AND EARLY DOMESTICATION

The history of *canis lupus familiaris* (friendly wolf dog) has been studied using mitochondrial DNA, which suggests that wolves and dogs split into different species around 100,000 years ago. Human efforts to domesticate the dog probably began 35,000 years ago. Although it has long been thought that the original location for the domestication of dogs was in East Asia, recent research suggests that it was more likely in what now comprises Europe. European domestication evidence shows that humans and dogs probably became occasional partners 30,000 years ago. The oldest consistent evidence found for a more interactive relationship is 14,000 years ago when dogs and people began to work together symbiotically, through the human sharing of food and shelter in return for dogs' assistance with hunting, herding, and guarding.

In modern Germany and Sweden, human burial sites showed interment of dogs with people 13,000 years ago. In the U.S., Danger Cave in Utah featured the first evidence of dogs buried with human remains—and dates to 11,000 years ago. Siberian regions have dog burial sites from 6,200 years ago and it appears that human companions gave their dogs ceremonial funerals and buried them in formal cemeteries.

NOMADIC LIFE

Once domesticated and befriended, dogs traveled with nomadic human tribes all around the world. Their relationships with people evolved into emotional companions as well as working partners, which benefited the survival of both species. Dogs assisted with hunts of prey that was larger than humans could have tackled alone. They guarded campsites from intruders—both other human tribes and wild animals. When people began keeping flocks of other domesticated animals such as sheep, goats, and cattle, dogs helped herd and guard those food animals, which helped make human life easier and less risky—because it was more practical to slaughter a domestic cow for food than to hunt a wild buffalo.

Dogs then traveled with their new "packs"—the nomadic human tribes. Dogs were able to physically and cognitively adjust to new locations, as their people were. When people migrated around the world, the most common animal companion was the dog—even before horses were domesticated as beasts of burden.

Eventually ancient people turned to farming and staying in place for longer periods of time, and dogs complied as well. Their intelligence, adaptability, and quick ability to fulfill human needs, in both work and emotional criteria, kept them at people's sides through the millennia of human social development.

DOG-HUMAN SOCIAL DEVELOPMENT

Contemporary dog owners probably never think of how their dog came to be a domesticated companion. How many Shih Tzu, Chihuahua, or Bichon owners contemplate their lap dog's ancestry? How did the Saint Bernard, the Greyhound, the Labrador Retriever, or the Rat Terrier come into being? It is mind boggling to realize that all dogs descended from ancient wild wolf stock.

Ancestor meets progeny.

Although recent molecular evidence shows that dog species are descended from the gray wolf, many modern dog breeds seem to have little in common with each other, or wolves. Years of selective breeding by humans have resulted in the speedy artificial evolution of dogs into many different types (for example, the Maltese vs. the Newfoundland). There are at least 150 different "pure" breeds and an infinite number of mixes. Today, dogs live with people in environments that range from primitive rainforests to sophisticated urban concrete jungles—yet it has only been within the last 175 years that all the major dog breeds have been controllably bred for specific human needs and markets.

THE VICTORIANS (1837–1901) AND THE EDWARDIANS (1901–1910)

British Queen Victoria was a passionate dog lover, and it was during her reign that formalized dog shows began as an aristocratic sport. Although dogs had been bred by humans for work characteristics (temperament, trainability, physical stamina, etc.), breeding for specific physical characteristics that had become aesthetically "fashionable," not practical, began in earnest during the Victorian era. This trend continued into the reign of Victoria's son, King Edward. Consequently, from the 1880s to around the turn of the last century, Western dogs came in from the cold—where they had been living in barns, yards, and sheds—and became pampered pets in upper-class human homes. The phenomenon of the pampered Victorian show dog brought life-on-a-leash to city dogs, although working dogs still ran free and proliferated in country environments.

Victorian Lady and her lap dog.

Working dogs were distinguished by docked (cut-off) tails, whereas nonworking pet dogs were fully tailed. This practice was made popular by nineteenth-century Europeans because a working dog was considered a tool of the trade (e.g., herding, guarding, hunting) and was not taxed. Pet dogs were thought of as luxuries—owned by the wealthy and living on aristocratic laps indoors—and were therefore taxed. To make the distinction between pet dog and working tool, the docked tail was an obvious and easy-to-see characteristic for the traveling tax assessor. Although many dogs continued to work in various trades alongside their human partners, more dogs, especially new smaller breeds, became uniquely and exclusively companions, with little expected from them except devotion and sociable presence.

The Industrial Revolution to World War II

The Industrial Revolution in the developed world resulted in the mass migration of people to cities. When people migrated from rural farm life to live in clustered tenements around factories, they obtained year-round work (as opposed to seasonal agricultural work), and they were out of their homes for long hours. Confined in crowded, noisy congestions of human populations—called "human zoos" by British anthropologist Desmond Morris—dog life had to conform to each owner's lifestyle. Dogs' lives were changed forever.

Former generations of dogs lived on farms and ranches, ran free, and had work guarding homesteads, tending livestock, assisting in hunting for mutual food sources and accompanying their owners as they performed chores on isolated properties. But when people migrated to cities, dogs were left alone the majority of the day and were confined in small yards or row homes. Dogs lost their own work. Today's dogs, regardless of breed, rarely work. Dogs' new main job evolved into companionship, not herding, guarding, hunting, or vermin killing.

From 1917 to 1946, World War I, the Great Depression, and World War II saw pet dog ownership drop because (1) unemployed people could not afford luxuries such as pets; (2) there was a huge increase in city-dweller homelessness; and (3) men, the primary breadwinners of families, were unemployed or off to war, leaving pet ownership an unstable, unaffordable, and inconvenient responsibility for family left behind in the United States as well as family living in the midst of the conflicts on the European continent. It was also during the wars that American families were encouraged to "donate" their pet dogs to the war effort, supposedly to help soldiers in combat.

The German army had hundreds of war dogs ready to deploy for World War II, having continued to breed and train them after their use in World War I. The Americans had let their use of Army dogs fade out, so when war was declared following the attack on Pearl Harbor in 1941, the call went out to citizens to patriotically give their family pet to the "war effort." Most of these docile, friendly pets were not trainable for the rough techniques then used by the armed forces. Of those that did make the cut for various jobs as sentries, scouts, messengers, or mine detectors in the "Dogs for Defense" system, many did not return. Some did make it back to the U.S. and were reunited with their families or retired with their military handlers.

POST-WORLD WAR II

When World War II ended, the following economic boom years of the 1950s brought the American suburban sprawl that housed thousands of returning soldiers and their new families. Dogs not only made a comeback as pets, but became status symbols—illustrating that the "head of the family" could not only support a wife, children, home, vehicle, and leisure time, but also myriad pets. The U.S. baby-boom generation of children became the first to be raised with pets such as dogs and cats as commonplace household fixtures in a burgeoning middle-class population. These animals were housed as companions, not contributing workers—a new phenomenon in the human/dog relationship in North America.

This is when history's largest increase in dog breeding occurred, of purebreds as well as mixed breeds. Most suburban neighborhoods frequently housed unintended litters of puppies due to the lack of widespread spaying and neutering. Most boomer children obtained their first dog from a neighbor. But as the human population exploded, even local sources for pets fell behind in the supply/demand chain. Hence, the up-and-coming businesses of puppy/kitten mills and retail pet stores. Farmers who were paid to not produce food, due to abundances, instead turned to mass breeding of pet animals to earn income. Former pens, outbuildings, and chicken and pig coops were stuffed with pregnant dogs and cats. Retail pet stores popped up in every neighborhood shopping center and offered not only puppies and kittens, but fish, turtles, hamsters, mice, birds, etc.

European countries lagged in affluence as they rebuilt shattered cities and lifestyles following the war, but eventually they caught up to American baby-boom generational trends.

THE AGE OF INFORMATION IN THE WESTERN WORLD

In America, the current Age of Information finds another huge uptick in pet dog ownership. As companions to their owners, dogs fill the void of traditional relationships people once depended on coworkers and family members for. The current high-tech society has resulted in people who only connect with each other online and in remote chat rooms or social media. The steady loyalty of a dog that is always at one's side is often the only live contact today's professional can routinely count on. More and more working people move around the large mainland to where jobs are available and leave behind long-standing human support systems—but do take their dogs to the cities of their new professional opportunities. Dogs' roles as companions are especially important in the new trend of telecommuting because many workers remain isolated in their homes during the work week. Without the constant socialization of an on-site office, technologically dominated positions leave workers without exposure to other people for many hours every day during the work week.

With the aging and retirement of the record-breaking baby-boom generation, increasing numbers of older people remain in their suburban and urban homes, even after children leave and a spouse dies. If they do move to senior group residences, many of those communities allow pets.

Also, increasing numbers of people of all ages choose to live alone, rather than with families, spouses, or roommates. In 2017, the United States Census Bureau reported that a record number of adults were not married. More than 110 million residents were divorced, widowed, or had always been single—more than 45 percent of all Americans aged 18 or older. The number of people living without a spouse or partner rose to 42 percent in 2017, up from 39 percent a decade ago.

Living alone is becoming more popular globally as well. In an analysis of a half-century of data (1960–2011) from 78 nations around the world, psychology researcher Henri C. Santos and his colleagues found that the popularity of living alone "grew significantly for 83 percent of the countries with relevant data."

Hence, the professional and personal environments of many people have once again partially returned to homebound isolation, just as it once was on farms. Perhaps the current rise in dog ownership reflects the renewed human need for companionship while working or in retirement. Recent research results have shown the mental and physical health benefits of pet companionship, and people of all ages and lifestyle choices continue to keep dogs. In fact, *Canis lupus familiaris*, the "friendly wolf dog," has become the second most common mammal in Western society, only outnumbered by *Felis catus,* the pet cat. Consequently, regardless of where people live, dogs can fit into peoples' lives, whereas other people sometimes do not, or cannot.

What kind of environments do companion dogs end up occupying? As the human species increases in numbers, and as farm life wanes in the wake of more complicated societies, what domiciles are dogs forced to live in? Let us now turn to how modern companion dogs live and what they need in those lifestyles from the people they remain devoted to.

TWO

CONTEMPORARY LIFESTYLES
OF DOGS AND PEOPLE

Urban, Suburban and Rural Environments

Most dogs and their people reside in urban or suburban environments. Few live in open country habitats. Dogs continue to be numerous in all human habitats, however, because they have become companions that share our lives no matter where, or how, we live. What are the pros and cons to these lifestyles for our dogs?

Urban or inner-city homes include apartments, condos, or small houses with no—or small—outside yards. Dogs that live in such abodes rarely live a natural dog life of running, playing, hunting or being free of constant human control due to fences and leashes. They walk on contrived substrates such as concrete, asphalt or artificial indoor-flooring surfaces. When outside, urban dogs must remain on leashes to keep safe in the face of many obstacles that country dogs are not exposed to.

City dogs need exercise every day.

Traffic, whether it is motor vehicles, bicycles, or human legs, presents dangers and often a scary view for the average dog. Everything is bigger, higher and larger than most dogs' level of eyesight. Their sensitive noses suffer from car exhaust, smog, garbage, housecleaning and yard chemicals. Their ears are bombarded by never-ending roars, squeals, sirens, home electronics, and human voices. Other environmental hazards are also a threat to dogs' health, and they abide in continual need of protection from the people they live with and trust. Artificial lighting and unusual human lifestyle hours disrupt a dog's natural biorhythms of sleep and wakefulness. Physical activity is dependent on the owner's whims, as are feeding schedules.

Suburban dog-human partnerships are a little better off than urban ones, because the dogs involved usually reside in larger, free-standing homes that include some sort of outside yard access. Greenbelts and parks offer more space and less noise to sensitive and alert dog senses. These environmentally green substrates—areas featuring grasses, dirt fields, trees and ponds—allow for more natural dog exercise. Open areas also offer life to undomesticated animals, such as deer, coyotes, rabbits, raccoons, foxes, skunks, prairie dogs, rats, and mice. Dogs rarely come across these sights and smells in the inner city.

Time with your dog(s) can be relaxing and scenic.

Sometimes neighborhood off-leash dog parks provide more spacious and fenced running/playing areas. There, for a few moments a week, a dog can be free of the constant physical restraint by her person, safe and able to engage in inherent dog behaviors with other dogs, and learn about her environment naturally. Consequently, dogs that spend their lives on leashes miss out on satisfaction of crucial exploratory instincts, do not develop inherent problem-solving abilities, and often experience anxiety when their trusted human controller is absent.

Fewer and fewer people, and therefore dogs, live in **rural** settings where a dog can run free with real abandonment on truly organic grounds of all indigenous substrates and flora. Dogs rarely have to work as they once did as life partners of farmers and ranchers because machinery has displaced them.

But regardless of where people take dogs to share their lives, dogs' ability to adapt and their devotion to people remains their most imperative contribution to human society. There are as many dog match options as there are human personality types. Lifestyles, locations, individual energy levels and aesthetic desires such as colors and coat type can result in a dog for everyone.

Because of the huge variance of sizes, activity levels, and other selected dog-breed characteristics and availability, dogs will continue to be partnered with people in city environments.

This book will be concerned with both the urban and suburban dog's life. How can a responsible, caring owner help his or her dog enjoy life while remaining safe and not becoming a nuisance or danger to other dogs and people?

THREE

WHAT DOGS NEED

WHAT DOGS NEED IN URBAN
AND SUBURBAN LIFESTYLES

Dogs' needs may seem simple on the surface, but delivering those needs safely and completely must concern every responsible owner. Dogs' main requirements, outside of basic sustenance (food and water), include companionship, shelter, medical care, as well as the most frequently neglected needs—physical exercise and mental stimulation. Exercise and mental stimulation will be our focuses in this book.

In *Animals Make Us Human: Creating the Best Life for Animals*, Dr. Temple Grandin and cowriter Catherine Johnson discuss what animals need to be emotionally happy.

"The animal welfare movement has been thinking about animals' mental welfare at least since the 1960s. That's when the British government commissioned the Brambell Report on intensive animal production. Intensive animal production means very big farms raising large numbers of animals for slaughter or egg production in very small spaces compared to traditional farms. The Brambell committee listed the five freedoms animals should have. The first three freedoms are about physical welfare, and the last two are about mental welfare:

1. Freedom from hunger and thirst
2. Freedom from discomfort
3. Freedom from pain, injury, or disease
4. Freedom to express normal behavior
5. Freedom from fear and distress

Dr. Grandin continues, "Dr. Jaak Panksepp, a neuroscientist at Washington State University who wrote the book *Affective Neuroscience* and is one of the most important researchers in the field, calls the core emotion systems (of all animals) the 'blue-ribbon emotions,' because they 'generate well-organized behavior sequences that can be evoked by localized electrical stimulation of the brain.'"

Dr. Grandin worked with Dr. Panksepp and documented that dogs have specific requirements to fulfill the fourth "blue-ribbon emotion"—the freedom to express natural behavior. One of the strongest natural behaviors every dog embodies is that of investigating her domain. Drs. Grandin and Panksepp termed this instinct "SEEKING" behavior.

Dr. Grandin writes, "Electrodes in the 'SEEKING' system (of the brain) make the animal start moving forward, sniffing, and exploring its environment. Dr. Panksepp says SEEKING is 'the basic impulse to search, investigate, and make sense of the environment.'"

Investigating environments is natural dog behavior.

When you walk your dog, her seeking instinct engages immediately. It is as crucial a part of the mental stimulation her mind requires as the physical stimulation her body needs. When you allow your dog to safely seek by scenting, seeing, hearing, exploring and wandering, you will ensure that her time in novel environments provides a multifaceted incentive to accompany you each time you set out. Forcing your dog to walk meekly and obediently at your side on a short leash throughout an entire walk negates the specific need your dog has to fulfill her seeking drive and can lead to her frustration—which may manifest in pulling, struggling against the leash, aggression towards other dogs or people, or conflicted avoidance of you when you approach with leash in hand. Emotional, cognitive, and physical exercise must go hand in hand (or paw in paw) for her needs to be fulfilled.

People manifest seeking behavior as well. For us, it is a combination of emotions people usually think of as "wanting something really good, looking forward to getting something really good, and curiosity, which most people probably don't think of as being an emotion at all," says Dr. Grandin.

"The wanting part of SEEKING gives you the energy to go after your goals, which can be anything from food, shelter, and sex, to knowledge, a new car, or fame and fortune. The looking-forward-to part of SEEKING is the Christmas emotion. When kids see all the presents under the Christmas tree, their SEEKING system goes into overdrive."

Dr. Grandin continues, "Curiosity is related to novelty. I think the orienting response is the first stage of SEEKING because it is attracted to novelty. When a deer or a dog hears a strange noise, he turns his head, looks, and pauses. During the pause, the animal decides, 'do I keep SEEKING, run away in fear, or attack?'

"New things stimulate the curiosity part of the SEEKING system. Even when people are curious about something familiar—like behaviorists being curious about animals, for instance—they can only be curious about some aspect they don't understand. They are SEEKING an explanation that they don't have yet. *SEEKING is always about something you don't have yet,* whether it's food and shelter, or Christmas presents, or a way to understand animal welfare." (Italics added for emphasis.)

Dr. Grandin says, "SEEKING is a very pleasurable emotion...the pleasure people feel when their SEEKING system is stimulated is the pleasure of looking forward to something good, not the pleasure of having something good. Jaak Panksepp says that SEEKING ... 'is the one system that helps animals anticipate all types of rewards.'"

In the case of a dog seeking rewards, unfettered investigation of her world manifests in sometimes dangerous ways. In city life, dogs cannot be turned loose to follow their curiosity due to safety needs that rival seeking desires. Consequently, dogs are kept in safe environments until their person allows them access to areas that they can safely explore. These allowances can take the form of controlled exercise, such as the dog walk.

Urban and Suburban Dog Exercise Outlets

Yards are the most common form of exercise outlet the modern dog has access to. Yet once beyond the playful puppy stage, most dogs do not voluntarily exercise themselves, unless a squirrel stimulates their prey drive, or someone walks past their territory and they announce a stranger's passing by running the fence and guard barking. Once their yard has become "old hat," dogs do not find their seeking drive satisfied and become complacent in investigatory activity.

Backyard dogs

Off-leash parks are growing in popularity but are still rare. Some are fenced, and some are merely open areas designated for dogs and people, with loosely defined and unsupervised boundaries. Unfortunately, if not physically confined by a leash or fence, dogs that are not well trained, or do not have close pack bonds (the wish to stay within a certain radius of the pack leader—you— or to at least "check in" frequently with their owners), often run off and enter dangerous areas and/or become lost. Due to their less frequent accessibility, and therefore novelty, plus their larger physical area, dog parks can provide good seeking outlets. The companionship of other dogs, both known and unknown, also adds to cognitive stimulation.

The most common exercise outlet for city dogs is the **dog walk,** on-leash with a human in tow. If a dog's person does not find the experience of a walk with his or her

Off-leash dog parks are new options

pet pleasurable, that pet will probably end up living a sedentary and unhealthy life. Yet walking together can be a bonding time, a time of undivided attention and affectionate companionship. It can also be a time of excellent cardiovascular benefit for both of you. Mutual exercise will keep dog and owner fit, healthy, and longer lived.

Part of making a dog walk pleasurable for you is a clear understanding of why this time with your pet is psychologically healthy as well as physically important. What makes the dog walk pleasurable for your dog is the time spent with you, the physical dissipation of energy, and the mental stimulation of processing sensory stimuli through her eyes, ears, and nose (seeking).

When dogs exercise through a lengthy walk, they fully empty their bowels and bladders, whereas in a yard or confined in a crate or house with only short periods outside, dogs retain urine, which can lead to urinary tract infections. Living a sedentary life, being rarely aroused, and often being trained to defecate inside—especially when living in high-rise apartments or confined in a crate or pen—could lead to longer retention times of fecal material prior to evacuation, with resultant inflammation of the bowels. Physical activity also improves circulation and prevents lymphangiectasia, the accumulation of lymph seen in some forms of canine inflammatory bowel disease.

Studies show that inactive, overweight dogs are more prone to heart diseases and depression. Obese dogs will also be at risk for developing liver disease and osteoarthritis, as well as insulin resistance and diabetes.

The simple preventative for all these mental and physical woes can be as simple as a walk with a human. Exercise relieves boredom and therefore resultant destructive behaviors. Behaviorally, outside exposure to new stimuli, including people and other dogs, builds dog confidence and sociability. Dogs are, after all, highly social beings and do not thrive in isolated conditions. No matter how much love and attention you shower upon your canine friend, she will still need access to other dogs and people. Her social needs will assist you with yours as well, because it is easier to meet other people with dogs than without.

WHY SPEND TIME WITH A DOG?

Yes, walking a dog is a great way to get *our own* exercise. It is safer to walk with a dog than alone—especially if you are a woman. And yes, many of us walk our dogs for their benefit, as well as our own. A dog is a rare and unique creature—domesticated, but still attuned to the natural world. A companion dog can seem to open the door to that wild world more readily than the door would open to us alone. Dogs find fascination in things we would often just pass by. They force us to stop frequently, look around, and notice details in our environment. A sniffing dog subliminally stimulates us to subconsciously attempt to find what odor holds her interest. We may find ourselves taking deeper breaths and awakening to new scents that, without our dog's attention, we would pass by with no awareness or interest.

By their very nature—inquisitive, curious, focused—dogs invite us into their world of scent, sound, and sight, with their bubbling urgency to take everything around them into their noses, eyes, ears, and mouths. The companionship of an adoring dog fills the gaps left by other humans who fly through our lives with hardly a nod—much different from the deep, slow, concentrated stare of a devoted dog that watches our every move and seems to know our emotions before we do. Dogs are astute students of our body language, facial expressions, and voice cues. We will never share our lives with anyone else who is so purely alert to every fiber of our fallible humanness. Hence, spending time on a walk with a dog can be the highlight of any day, and surely a boost to a poor day.

Dog Walking Philosophy

Dog walking can be a quick in-and-out trip to give your dog a chance to relieve herself, an opportunity for both of you to stretch your legs, or an all-out heart-pumping workout session. A dog walk can also be a long, lingering, meander of soulful companionship and in-the-moment discovery of the world you share.

All chances to bring a dog and owner together are good, and not every venture outdoors needs to be a serious effort at aerobic exercise. On the contrary, most dogs prefer a chance to pee five hundred times, leave poop postcards, and spend as much time with you as they can manipulate. Their main goal seems to be to help us learn how to slow down and "smell the fire hydrant," as they do.

Being together is a reason for outings.

Most people face their daily routines as systematic, compartmentalized cubes of duty. Dogs face their day as if each activity has never been done, and they are as enthusiastic during their tenth urination as they were on their first. Sniffing the same tree is never boring to them—they approach it as though someone sneaked in and planted that tree in the middle of the previous night, just to surprise them. Every outing for a dog is thrilling and novel—and a reason for joyful exploration.

We could learn from our dogs' appreciation of simple pleasures and optimistic, investigative attitude. Instead, we snap on the leash as though anything would be better to do than take the same old spin around the same old block. We desensitize ourselves to nature and our dogs' joy by isolating ourselves under headphones of blaring music or carrying on nonurgent, and often pointless, cell phone discussions with other humans during the few minutes a day that our dogs have our companionship. We betray their loyalty and excited focus on us by purposefully ignoring them and turning our attention to whatever technological distraction we can afford. If our children, spouses, parents, coworkers, or friends treated us the way we treat our dogs when we were together, we would be hurt, furious, insulted, and less likely to accept another invitation from them.

But not our dogs! They treat every opportunity to share time with us as a golden occasion to bask in the glory of their gods and goddesses—us. They accept our lack of reciprocation of attention and love us still. Offer a dog a walk once and she will remember what the leash is for forever. She will also anxiously await each chance to walk out the door with you at her side.

DOG WALKING GOALS

So, before we move on, let us agree that every walk with our dogs should entail conscious efforts to be aware, be present, and to attend to them as they do us (in between each fascinating tree or shrub). Let us put away our mechanical devices and distracting thoughts. Let us head out with our best friends and see the world we inhabit together—as they do.

FOUR

DOG WALKING ESSENTIALS

EQUIPMENT NEEDED

Every project is easier with the right tools, and dog walking is no exception. The appropriate equipment for you and your dog will help make your time together more enjoyable and safer. There are more options now than ever before, and it can be confusing and expensive trying to find exactly what you both need. A personalized pet-supply store will offer knowledgeable staff who can work one on one with you and your dog to get you off on the right foot—and paw! Here are the basics:

1. Cloth Snap-On Collar

Cloth collars are more comfortable for dogs, especially in weather extremes. They are also more humane—dogs learn fear from choke-chain and metal-prong collars, not partnership. There is no reason to control your dog by collar jerking and, therefore, choking her. Secure snap-on clips are also safer: if a dog gets caught on something, it is quicker to unsnap a twisted collar than to get the choking dog to calm down enough to obtain the slack needed to unhitch a buckle collar. The faster you can release a tight collar, the less likely you are to be bitten by a frightened, panicked dog.

Before you purchase a collar, snap it together and pull on both sides to see if it will let go inappropriately. Good quality collars will not pop open with a slight bit of tension. Press the release clips and make sure they do pop open easily under tension from both sides of the collar, in case of emergency.

Never use a prong collar. Prongs are harsh, inhumane, uncomfortable, and dangerous for dogs. There is no way a prong or choke-chain collar can be quickly removed in an

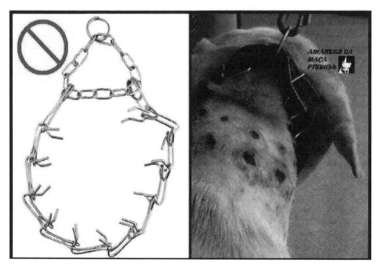

The nefarious prong collar is always dangerous.

emergency. A choke-chain or prong collar tells the world you do not have control over your dog—a negative statement that says more about you than your dog.

2. Identification Tags

Tags should clearly state your name, address and phone number, just in case your dog does get lost. Include rabies tags, tattoo ID, microchip registration and number, and medical alert information. Tags are more easily seen and can result in your lost dog being returned sooner than a trip to a vet or police station for microchip scanning, and resulting calls to your chip company for information about your whereabouts.

3. Microchip

If a collar comes off or your dog is stolen and her collar is removed, an identifying microchip implanted in her withers may be the key to getting her home again. Make sure you keep all your contact information up to date with your microchip company, your veterinarian who inserted the chip, and/or the shelter/rescue where you obtained your dog (especially if they inserted it). In many jurisdictions, you can also inform your local animal control department of your contact information, in case they pick up your lost dog.

4. Leash

Chain leashes can catch a tooth, a claw, or a finger, and they are hot in summer and cold in winter. Good-quality leather or tightly woven cloth/mesh leashes are best for three- to six-foot teaching leashes. A quality retractable leash with distance control options allows your dog the ability to seek and will be more fun for the educated dog.

5. Harness

Many people prefer to attach their leashes to harnesses instead of to collars. Dogs with short or injured necks, small dogs, short-snouted breeds and any dog that can easily slip out of a collar should be walked with a harness. Dogs that pull can be controlled better with no-pull harnesses, which spread the pressure of a stubborn or fearful pull over the dog's body, not the handler's shoulders, neck, and back.

6. Head Halter

Another excellent tool for the pulling dog, head halters work on the same premise as halters do on thousand-pound animals such as cattle and horses. When the

Snub-nosed boxers should never wear head gear.

leash is connected to the chin area of the halter, the pulling dog simply does a U-turn and ends up facing you—providing you with a great opportunity to redirect her behavior to something rewardable, without having your arm jerked. Brachycephalic dogs (dogs with short snouts, such as pugs, boxers, and bulldogs) should not use halters because of their already compromised breathing due to head shape. Head halters must never, ever be jerked, as they can cause severe damage to the dog's head and neck. But jerking any leash and collar (commonly called "pop-and-jerk" training) should not be done, regardless of the tools you have.

7. Poop Bags

Never leave your house without a fanny pack or pocketful of poop bags. Not only is leaving your dog's excrement socially rude, it is environmentally unsound. Coyotes, horses, cattle, rabbits, and prairie dogs eat vegetarian foods; therefore, their manure returns nutrients to the soil. Dogs eat protein, which when excreted, leaves behind dangerous chemicals. It has been estimated that a single gram of dog waste can contain 23 million fecal coliform bacteria, which are known to cause cramps, diarrhea, intestinal illness, and serious kidney disorders in humans. The Environmental Protection Agency (EPA) estimates that two days' worth of droppings from a population of 100 dogs (easily the population of the average dog park) would contribute enough bacteria to temporarily close a bay, and all watershed areas within 20 miles of it, to swimming and shell fishing. This sounds extreme, but it is safe to say that dog excrement is not safe. Even if you have no surface bodies of water nearby, underground aquifers are just as much at risk from seeping bacteria following rain or snowmelt penetration.

8. Supportive Walking Shoes (for you)
Discover which type of walking shoe is most appropriate for you—low-top tennies, high-top boots, or walking or running shoes. Inserts for arch support, cushioning, or any other accommodation for your foot issues will be important. Without feet and legs that are pain-free and comfortable, a dog walk will not be your favorite activity, which it should be.

9. Preparation for Weather (for you and your dog)
For You: Layers of clothing and appropriate material for your climate and time of year are a given. If you are too hot, cold, or wet, you will not want to spend time outdoors with your dog. Modern textiles offer a wide variety of materials for all weather—waterproof, breathable, sweat-wicking, windproof, and warm overcoats are available with minimal bulk. Protect your head, where substantial body heat escapes in winter, and where sunlight exposure can result in deadly skin cancers. Lightweight, leash-friendly gloves are important, especially when frostbite of naked fingers is possible. Supportive shoes or boots with good traction in mud or snow will protect your feet, ankles, knees, hips and back—while allowing you to keep up with an enthusiastic dog.
For Your Dog: If your dog has hair rather than fur with an undercoat, you may want to purchase weather gear for her too. Of course, you must remain aware of your

dog's comfort. Do not walk when it is above 85 degrees Fahrenheit, especially if it is humid. Dogs can only cool themselves through panting, which is not an efficient system. The same is true for extreme cold. Paws and ears are susceptible to frostbite, so do not go out for long in below-freezing temperatures. Humid cold, like humid heat, is more extreme and affects body systems faster than dry extremes. Wind chill should also be considered, for the way a temperature feels, rather than what it actually is, will the affect health, safety and comfort of both of you.

For You Both: Be especially mindful of thunderstorms and lightning. Many dogs are frightened of thunder, and indeed, they have no way of knowing the sky will not fall. Dogs cannot know the logical explanation for thunder, and if you try to empathize with your dog's perception of such a scary phenomenon, you will understand how startling a sudden boom, earth tremor and electrical air change can be. Lightning is also a bizarre and terrifying experience. Many dogs are panicked into escapism with both weather events, especially when they occur together. Not only is lightning alarming, but it is dangerous for both of you to be out in. Plan ahead and try to never get caught in violent rainstorms.

10. Training Treats

If your dog is in training (and all dogs should be, throughout their lives), always be prepared with her favorite reward. A fanny pack of small pieces of cheese or slices of hot dogs at the ready will speed up rewardable behaviors or distract from a questionable situation (for example, an oncoming bicyclist or feared stimulus).

If your dog is not food motivated, carrying a favorite toy for spontaneous play is also an excellent reward for desirable behavior.

11. Cell Phone
Carrying a cell phone is imperative these days. Although talking on the phone instead of attending to your dog is not wise, having an emergency communication device is important. Beware of using your phone for anything other than an emergency. Other dog walkers may not be aware, considerate, or intelligent enough to keep their dog safe and under control. If they are distracted, you could end up with dog-to-dog conflict, unless you are paying attention to your own dog's body posture, which you cannot if you are talking on your phone.

Having a phone with you is a safety tool best kept in your pocket until you absolutely need it. You may have occasion to call law enforcement for help with several possible scenarios (dog fights, wildlife encounters, accidents resulting in injury to yourself or your dog, or aggressive bicyclists).

12. Pepper Spray, Coyote Whistle, Air Horns, Other Noisemakers, and Flashlights
Understand what wild creatures you may run into around your own area. Regional wildlife will vary, but almost all areas in North America have coyotes, raccoons, skunks, foxes, and deer. Educate yourself in your own specialized wildlife by researching through your State Division of Wildlife. They will be the best resource for what works with each critter. We will discuss the most common possible scenarios.

There is some debate about whether coyotes react to pepper spray, but other wildlife and aggressive humans do. Many species of wild animals have learned to coexist with humans and domestic pets in urban and suburban areas. **Raccoons**, **skunks** and **foxes** are considered mesopredators and are mostly nocturnal. If you walk at night, especially after your work day and during the short winter months, you will have some likelihood of encountering them.

Coyotes are the top predator; they are often seen day or night and are of more concern to dog owners. Coyotes prefer no interaction with people but they will feel threatened by a fellow canid (your dog) in their territory. Educate yourself about this cousin of your dog, for they now occupy even the largest cities throughout North America. Hazing (to frighten coyotes away) is the preferred method to discourage interaction—both to keep a coyote from becoming too familiar with—and therefore habituated—to people and dogs, and to keep the coyote safe from humans. Coyotes are extremely intelligent, easily trained, and can tell people and dogs apart. Coyotes claim territorial areas and will see any dog as an interloper, which can result in conflicts.

Living peacefully with wild animals requires humans to respect their wildness, and hazing them will teach them to stay away from you and your dog. There are many tools for hazing such as yelling; throwing rocks; big, aggressive body posture; whistles; and air horns. Whistles emit shrill, loud, aversive squeals that can deter an overly curious wild animal, and they can work on aggressive loose dogs as well. Other noisemakers, such as small air horns or cans with pebbles inside, can be shaken to scare off wildlife and are especially handy if you happen to wander into a claimed territory of a denned fox or coyote parent. Pay attention if your Division of Wildlife or Parks Department has posted signs that coyote activity has been observed, or that known dens are in your walking area during the months of November through April (mating, denning, and pup-raising months). Coyotes are hard to see unless they want to be, and often that is right before they take hold of your dog. Dogs are usually considered competition for resources rather than a food source, and they will be dispatched quickly and quietly—before you can do anything. Smaller wild critters will be more likely to run away, unless they are injured, ill, or protecting young (pups/coyotes, kits/foxes, and skunks).

Stay out of known denning areas until the wild pups or kits are grown and out, able to hunt and wander with their parents. Coyotes and other wild animals are particularly devoted parents and will become aggressive if their families are endangered. Actual attacks on people by coyotes are far rarer than bites to humans by dogs, but your dog will be vulnerable and it is your responsibility to foresee danger and protect her. Raccoons are usually more aggressive than coyotes, especially with young in tow, so if you walk in the dark, use a flashlight to see what is around you. Raccoons usually avoid bright light and will hopefully be long gone by the time you and your dog arrive.

13. Camera

Cameras are increasingly important in this age of rudeness and litigiousness by humans. If there is any altercation between you, your dog and (1) other dogs, (2) insane people, (3) speeding bicyclists, or (4) runners who come up/through/around/at you and your dog, a filmed record will settle disputes. Remember, if someone accuses your dog of aggressive behavior and you are not at fault but have no record of the event, it will be the dog who pays the price (often with her life) in a court of law.

It is difficult to handle a frightened (fear-aggressive or cowering) dog, hang onto a leash, hold poop bags, and also take pictures. Consider a GoPro-type camera that is hands-free. Head- or body-mounted cameras are the best for continuous filming. If you have frequent conflicts in highly populated neighborhoods, parks, or trails, record your entire walk (make sure you have audio as well as video) so you do not have to struggle to turn the camera on. You can always erase an uneventful walk afterwards.

If most of your walk is without interference, you do not have to record. But if an incident begins, it takes a small movement to reach up and hit the "On" button and begin recording. When people are tempted to harass you but see the camera on your head or chest, mounted for easy access, they often think twice about approaching or accosting you. Ironically, most people are extremely nice when they believe they are being recorded! Whether you use a camera as a deterrent or actually need to record a conflict, the price of this technology can easily offset possible future legal costs. Plus, it is fun to watch your walk with your best friend again on a day you cannot get out.

14. Water Bottle and Collapsible Bowl

When there are no readily available water sources on your route, carry this most important resource. Dogs become dehydrated easily, particularly in extreme weather conditions. Their panting utilizes much of their body's water reserves. Their paw pads will also sweat when they are overheated. Heatstroke will seriously impair and can kill your dog quickly. Your own hydration is important too. If you walk for an hour or more, water is imperative for both of you, especially if walking conditions are in hot, humid, or exclusively sunny areas.

Also, if your dog injures herself, you can wash the site with water. If the injury occurs to a paw and you cannot carry your dog, frequent flushing may be adequate to avoid infection on the walk home.

15. First Aid Supplies

If you plan a long walk, especially in areas that you are not familiar with, always carry water, gauze, stretch wrap, disinfectant, scissors and medical tape in a kit you can stow in a fanny pack or backpack. Never assume your dog will not stick her nose somewhere it should not be. If you live where venomous snakes or spiders reside (and they do, even in cities), ask your veterinarian for antivenom, if it is available. There are organizations that offer to "snake proof" your dog. They travel around seasonally and are a knowledgeable resource. If you have the opportunity to take a snake avoidance course with your dog, do so. Dogs are curious about snakes and are often bitten before a person behind them even knows there is an issue.

Study up on the area you and your dog will be exploring, and be prepared—before the worst happens. Snake bites can happen in a flash, but the long walk back to your house or car carrying a heavy dog, and then a far drive to an emergency vet, may be avoided if you have your dog close to you and under constant supervision. Do not assume urban or suburban areas or dog parks are danger-free. Although snakes prefer less trafficked areas, they are reasonably plentiful in suburban gardens, especially when there are open spaces nearby that will provide mice, voles, and other food resources. Beware of rock gardens that provide a habitat for snakes. Spiders reside everywhere.

16. Protein Snacks or Food

Long walks in open areas, in parks, on suburban trails, or even through city neighborhoods will require nourishment for both you and your dog. Pack kibble or any other specialty dog energy food or snack for short hikes. Hydrating canned or another type of wet food for your dog would be better than dry food on long treks, although you must make sure it does not spoil. Dogs will wander many more miles than a human walks, even on-leash. We tend to stay straight in our directions while dogs zig-zag wherever their noses take them. They use up far more energy and they are powering four legs, not just two.

Your Dog's Physical Comfort and Safety

Your dog's natural body temperature is 101 degrees Fahrenheit, higher than our 98.6 degrees. Dogs cannot tolerate heat well, so do not overstress your dog with vigorous exercise in extreme heat. Avoid routes in direct sunlight and seek shady areas. Do not walk on concrete or pavement; paw pads can easily be burned on hot days. Find dirt or grass to protect paws. Be especially aware of a puppy's or an older dog's comfort because they have even less ability to regulate their body temperature than middle-aged dogs.

Be aware of how your dog experiences temperature and weather. Short dogs can easily be overcome by the heat radiating off the ground or become sick from low-lying ozone emissions if you are near automobile traffic. Small dogs will also be closer to frozen ground and will feel the chill that radiates from ice and deep snow before a taller dog will. If you own a small dog, lie down on the ground and then lift your head to the same level as hers. Feel what she feels. Roll over and look around—the world is a mighty big place to a small dog. Think twice before you expect her to charge through two feet of snow or be ignored on a hot day's walk over concrete next to a busy roadway.

Brachycephalic dogs have especially significant breathing issues. Because their nasal passages and mouths are exceptionally short, they do not have the ability to heat incoming air the way that longer-snouted or longer-mouthed dogs can. Be especially careful of walking brachycephalic dogs in extreme heat or cold.

Be cognizant of your dog's age, physical fitness level and ability to navigate terrain. Unforgiving concrete sidewalks or large hills can pose difficult challenges to an older, arthritic dog. Your walk should revolve around your dog's abilities and comfort, not your own. Take frequent rests, provide water and food, and cater to your dog's ability to return. Always keep in mind that however far and difficult your route out, your dog must also have the stamina to return. If you want a more vigorous workout than your dog can handle, go alone or with other people.

FIVE

DOG WALKING COMMUNICATION

POLITE AND HUMANE TRAINING

Although leashes and collars are tools of every dog walk, especially in high-traffic urban environments, their main use is to keep your dog in your immediate vicinity. Short or long leashes are tools to keep your dog relatively close, safe, and controlled from wandering off. Leashes are not steering wheels or instruments for human ego-driven control issues. Dragging a dog around a corner with no attempt to alert her of a change in your direction is rude, confusing, and possibly frightening to her. Pulling a dog out of danger may be necessary on occasion but most of the time, potential oncoming interactions will allow you enough time to prepare your dog with appropriate verbal commands of direction. Yanking and choking your dog via the leash is not necessary, or enjoyable for her.

There are better ways to communicate to your dog as you enjoy each other's company on a walk. Use your leash as a safety device only.

For example, as the tallest person in the partnership (and since you probably will not have your head down sniffing like she will), you will see oncoming danger—such as a speeding bicyclist—before your dog does. Instead of a sudden jerk on your leash, call your dog to your side and out of the way of the bike, and give your dog plenty of time to respond, if possible. If the bicyclist is coming too fast, move your own body close to your dog and tighten your leash only enough to keep her near. Moving your own body can be faster than jerking and dragging

Always be aware of your surroundings
and protect your dog.

a distracted dog across a path. Having both of you close together and holding still, as one unit, will give the bicyclist more room to go around you, regardless of what side of the path you are on.

If your dog finds an inviting smell and you see it is a piece of rotten food or other potentially harmful substance, a trained *leave it* command (see page 79) will be more humane than a leash pop. If you are relaxed and able to let your dog out to the full length of a retractable leash, it makes sense to have a release word so your dog understands she is free to leave your side and wander. Alternatively, it is as important for your dog to understand when you need her to come close or freeze where she is and remain motionless until danger passes.

Dogs have the potential to understand many verbal cues. Jerking the leash teaches the dog that you are unpredictable and to be ignored or, worse, feared. Verbal cues teach your dog to trust you, and they encourage her attention and response.

During the time we spend with our dogs, verbal communication is the most common human tool for teaching the dog what we expect—and gives the dog the chance to use her brain, react, and be rewarded for the proper response. Hand and body signals also communicate to your dog and, with time, you can pair both verbal and physical cues for clearer communication. But for times when your dog is not looking directly at you for hand signals, audible verbal commands are necessary.

Dogs trust physical body language before verbal communication because they are nonverbal animals. Try to never allow your body to contradict what your voice says. If such contradiction takes place, understand that your dog will respond more readily to whatever your body language says to her. Do not correct a dog for a wrong interpretation when your body and your verbal cues do not synchronize. In such circumstances, it is your own fault for the communication snafu, not your dog's. Pay attention to your physical cues. If necessary, attend a dog training class with a knowledgeable instructor. A professional trainer will be able to see in your own movements what you do not. An observant instructor will be able to help you make sure your body and your voice cues go together.

Smooth communication between your dog and you will make your relationship deeper. Being two separate entities that do not pay attention to each other results in an empty relationship and is not fair to your dog, who so desperately wants to connect with you and understand what you want.

Communication is also vital to the safety of your dog. If a dangerous situation is imminent, a proper command and your dog's compliant performance can save her from injury. Your walk together will be more enjoyable if you understand and trust each other through practiced, flowing communication.

USEFUL WORDS FOR HUMANE COMMUNICATION

While your dog and you get to know each other, or if you have had your dog for a while and want to try to better your on-leash communication, the everyday words you can use are simple. The famous British dog trainer Barbara Woodhouse once said that the average dog can have the same vocabulary as a five-year-old child. That was before recent research, in which many studies continually show the high level of cognitive ability dogs possess. It is easy to find basic obedience classes in your area, either online or via books. I have never found a course that teaches specific dog-walking communication, but learning to teach your dog basic obedience and how to utilize timely rewards can be translated into anything you want to teach her.

A basic obedience class will teach you how to show your dog your desired response to a command and how to reward that response positively. Because dog-to-dog socialization is important, I encourage you to take classes in person with your pup. Once you grasp the concepts of teaching command/proper response/positive reward, you can then transfer that knowledge to your daily dog walks. Fortunately, the intelligence of dogs shows they are eager, willing, and able to pick up words with repetition.

Repetition and consistency are the keys. Every dog (unless cognitively or physically incapable) can pick up the basics with your patient teaching. Communicating with and teaching a dog is not very different from raising a human toddler. Consistency in your requests and the words you use to ask for compliance are crucial to avoiding canine confusion.

Here is a list of the words and commands that will be useful on an everyday walk with your canine friend:

1. **Collar:** When a dog hears this word, she will know she is being prepared and should sit still to allow the collar, head halter or harness to be put on.

2. **Leash:** This word tells the dog she is going somewhere; she should be taught to sit still for

attachment, regardless of where she is or how excited she is to be going.

3. **With me:** A clear communication that you are attached to the other end of the leash and that manners will be expected.

4. **Walk on:** For beginning the walk or for starting up after a halt in progression.

5. **Stop:** Freeze in place. Can be an alarm command; can be combined with a sit/look-for-further-direction behavior; can then be combined with a *wait* command.

6. **Sit:** A command for a neutral body posture in case of oncoming dogs; a controlled posture for collaring and leashing, or waiting politely for further commands.

7. **Wait:** Stop forward motion. More casual than the *stop* command; not as long as a *stay*.

8. **Left:** Turn left.

9. **Right:** Turn right.

10. **This way:** No definitive directional turn, yet a gradual change in direction; watch my body. Can be paired with an arm/hand signal toward the direction to go in.

11. **Down:** Lie down.

12. **Leave it:** Do not touch, smell, or pay attention to (things, dogs, or people).

13. **Take it:** Okay to eat, mouth, play with, or approach.

14. **Come:** The MOST IMPORTANT COMMAND OF ALL; come to me immediately!

15. **Eh-eh-eh:** Stop what you are doing and look to me for further command.

16. **Go:** Move ahead, move away, or go wherever your hand/arm signal points.

17. **Go around it:** I am on the opposite side of that pole, tree, bench or other obstacle, so you must figure out how to untangle yourself and come in my direction.

18. **Come-on:** Come to my area. Not as formal or urgent as *come* directly to my location.

19. **Close:** Tighten up distance and get closer to my legs. Can be repeated to bring the dog closer.

20. **Free dog:** These are release words that give the dog permission to leave the previous command; they let the dog know formal compliance is over. (You can make up any word to use but avoid *okay*. That word is used too frequently in human communications.)

21. **Good Puppy, Nice Work, or Excellent:** Words of praise; reward for correct decisions and proper performance; periodic positive reinforcement for calm, ongoing behavior; encouragement for nothing in particular. Words are less important than tone of voice.

Note: Any and all of these words can be accompanied by, or replaced with, hand signals as your communication skills grow. I encourage the use of both verbal and hand signal fluency (complete comprehension) because as your dog companion ages, her hearing can become impaired. If she is unable to hear, you will be able to continue to communicate through hand signals. This will keep her

engaged as she ages, for many dogs will emotionally withdraw or become intensely clingy when
they feel they are losing sensory connection with
you in their later years.

A word about *No*. Avoid this empty word. *No* provides no direction, incentive, or desire to pay attention
for the dog. It is overused and has no meaning, especially
if not accompanied by guidance to a rewardable behavior.
You can use *no* as a noise marker to stop an undesirable
behavior, although the sound *eh-eh-eh* is more generic
and is not as commonly used in everyday language that
your dog may hear other people use. If your dog hears *no*
from other people around her, she may look for guidance,
respond with curiosity, or even cringe in anticipation of
correction. But when none is forthcoming from any person, she will learn to ignore (if no rewardable behavioral
request is made), or fear (interpreting as unpredictabil-
ity), any person who says it.

Even if you, her trainer, use the word in common
conversation with other people, she will hear it and may
become confused. The word *know* will catch her attention—she has no way to comprehend that the two identi-
cal sounds mean different things. Human conversation-
alists move so quickly through the sounds they make
that they rarely, if ever, consider the dog's ability to pick
out familiar words, even when the rest of human vocal
expressions are just garbledy-gook. It is best to avoid this
word and train yourself to train your dog with specific
words for specific actions that are not commonly used in
random, everyday conversations your dog may hear.

SIX

DOG WALKING ETIQUETTE

Etiquette means "manners." In today's extremely casual society, few people are raised with the strict manners and moral codes of previous generations. Poorly trained people make for poorly trained dogs. Basic manners equate to the old adage, "Treat others as you would have them treat you." Awareness, common sense, and consideration for others should be within your own behavioral repertoire. If you are lax in socially accepted manners, your dog will be too. It is every dog owner's responsibility to teach their dog what is needed for that animal to be welcomed into the human environment she is forced to live within.

When you are in public and on a walk, be aware of your dog's manners as well as your own. Here is a list of courteous rules—some concerning your behavior and some concerning your dog's behavior (which you should have under control). You can probably add to these basic guidelines, depending on your environment (where you and your dog are), your social context (what people/animals are around you), and the immediate need for control of your own, or your dog's, behavior.

Choose the right leash length for each activity.

LEASH LENGTH

Always keep your dog on a leash length that you can control. If your leash is too long and your dog is uneducated, you can be pulled off your feet if your dog decides to investigate something and gets the chance to get a good run at it. If you are walking more than one dog, be sure you can handle the lengths of all your leashes and avoid tangles. If your leashes are tangled and you must respond to an emergency, such as an oncoming speeding bicyclist, you will not have time to sort through the knot and pull your dogs to safety. This is where reliable voice command obedience comes in handy for you and your dogs.

Although loose-leash compliance is the ultimate goal, the leash is your lifeline to your canine friend. The leash keeps your pup close enough to be under your protective eye and active supervision. In an emergency, you can pull your dog out of harm's way. In the case of a fearful or unsure elderly dog, slight tension on the line between you can reassure her that you are there for her—that she is free to explore, but that you are just steps away if she needs help. Older off-leash dogs can become confused and frightened if their aging senses cannot tell where you are. Early stage dementia in dogs can cause wandering or anxiety-driven fleeing—mad running away from you and into danger. Never let an older dog off-leash if you know her sight, hearing, or cognitive processing is compromised. You may even have to abandon a lengthy retractable leash for a six-foot leash to provide your dog with the psychological comfort of your proximity. There are times when a harness and leash held with slight tension can help keep a falling, elderly dog from complete collapse. Also, as an elderly dog's hindquarters weaken, you can "sling walk" her with a front-end leash and a supportive rear-end sling with handle straps to keep her moving as long as possible. Devising ways to keep an old dog up and moving is beneficial for her on many levels.

For young dogs, teaching sessions should be on a leash no longer than six feet so that you can control your dog's actions and teach success, not failure due to lack of control. Once your dog and you are fluent and reliable in verbal/hand signal communication, the leash becomes a tool that (1) keeps your dog within your vicinity, (2) keeps you both compliant with local leash laws, and (3) keeps you both safer from the myriad hazards that you may encounter on a walk (see Chapter Seven). At this point, you can gradually increase length of leash freedom, all the while proofing your dog for obedience. Only when she is constantly able to perform at greater distance, should you allow her the freedom of a fully retractable leash (usually twenty feet long).

BASIC COMMANDS

Teach your dog basic obedience skills, such as *sit, come, leave it, off* (no jumping up on people or other dogs), *this way* and *with me* (pay attention to the direction my body is moving), and how to walk on a short leash—before you take her into public areas. With multiple distractions around, basic commands will be hard enough to enforce if your dog is not fluent (that is, she knows exactly what each word means and that the behavior is the same, regardless of location).

Out of a confined area, such as her home or yard, any inexperienced dog will react with enthusiasm, excitement, and interest in exploring (seeking). However, your relationship should be strong enough that your dog honors your leadership so that when you give a command, she responds enthusiastically. Obedience commands should be taught as fun games that *always* end in enticing rewards such as food treats, a toy, and verbal and physical praise. Consequently, when your dog is challenged by an enticing distraction (scampering squirrels, bouncing bunnies, stinky tidbits on the trail) that subverts her attention from you, her attention can be reliably regained. Practice all the basic commands on gradually increasing leash lengths so your dog's responses are dependable, regardless of her distance from you. Once your dog is trained, fluent in her knowledge, and trustworthy in her responses, a retractable leash can be appropriate.

JUMPING ON PEOPLE

Never allow your dog to jump on people. It is a bad habit that most people on the receiving end do not enjoy. It is natural for dogs to greet each other by jumping up and licking lips. Understand that although this is natural dog behavior, your dog must learn to conform to behavior that is welcome in the human-dominated public areas she inhabits. Jumping up can also be dangerous for people being greeted, if they are not expecting it, are frail, or have an innate fear of dogs. A dog that jumps up on people is an example of bad manners—hers and yours. Teach your dog how to be a calm and welcome diplomat for her species.

Teaching your dog that jumping up is inappropriate in the human world is doable and not difficult. Once again, begin at home in a quiet environment where you can attain her undivided attention. Place a treat low over her head and move your hand forward over her back. As she looks up at the treat (do not hold it high enough to entice jumping up to get it), her rear end should drop into the sit position. If she already knows *sit,* you do not have to use the word. If she does not know *sit,* use the word.

Every time she approaches you in greeting, be ready to reinforce an immediate *sit* in front of you by carrying treats to teach and then reward.

Once fluent, proof your dog with other people. Give the people treats for your student, and explain what you want them to do. When you bring your dog into their vicinity and she wants to greet them, have them copy the reinforcement for sitting. The dog should only receive treats if all four feet and her rear end are on the ground. Be careful to not mistime your treat/reinforcement when your dog either has already jumped or is about to jump up. Repetition with strangers as well as people she knows should prove to your dog that the only way to obtain attention is to sit and wait politely for it. When your training is successful, every greeting your dog wishes to bestow on a new human should result in a quick, snap sit. If she is sitting, she cannot jump. If she knows she will only receive solicited attention when she is in the sit position, she will use this position instead of guessing what people want and jumping, running, or pulling for attention.

PASSING OTHERS ON WALKS

If you and your dog are walking and must pass another person from behind, let the person ahead of you know you are coming. Simply say, "Excuse us. We are behind you and about to pass on your left." Your voice gives the other person a chance to locate you and your dog. Giving notice of your location is polite and lets the person who is slower gather his or her wits before a sudden appearance of a dog at their side startles them. Your friendly voice to a stranger also tells your dog that the person is no danger, so she will not be motivated to exhibit protective behavior as you go around.

Speak and curve around when passing pedestrians from behind.

When you pass, keep your dog close to you, on the opposite side of you from the person. Speak to your dog in cheery tones to (1) keep her attention on you, not the stranger, and (2) alleviate any possible fear your dog may have toward the stranger, which could cause aggression, lagging, or jerking away from your path. Having your dog on the opposite side of you will give her an obstacle to go around (you) to get to the other person, so lunging or jumping up are more difficult for her and control is easier for you.

Again, you are her leader, and she should trust your judgment in a peaceful, purposeful passing of another pedestrian. Give your dog and the other person a respectful distance as you go by. This is especially important if you are walking more than one dog.

Changing Direction

Do not jerk your dog when you change direction. Give your dog a word for your directional change (*left, right,* or *this way),* and give the dog a chance to respond, without a sudden choke. Multiple on-leash dogs can learn to respond to your directional commands in the same manner as a school of fish. Often it is easier to teach a new dog when more experienced and already trained dogs accompany her.

When beginning this training, it is easier to train one dog at a time. Hold treats low on the side the dog is walking on while you hold her leash in your opposite hand. Your treat hand should be in front of her nose, next to your leg, to teach her to watch your leg direction. Eventually, when you change directions, she should automatically attend to your legs as well as your voice.

STOPPING

When you must stop (at corners of busy streets, to allow someone to cross in front of you, or to greet someone you know), tell the dog to *stop, sit,* and *wait.* When your dog is contained, turn your attention to the reason you had to stop. Always keep an eye on your dog and be aware of her impending boredom (e.g., if you are chatting with another person). Do not let the dog fail in her behavior by expecting long waits, sits, or downs. Move on before the dog "breaks" command. Teach success, not failure. Do not take the fun out of your time together by repeated corrections.

To teach the emergency *stop* command, you must start on a short leash. When you distinctly and sharply say, "Stop," cease your own movement. If your dog is not paying attention, she will continue to move forward and, therefore, self-correct by hitting the end of the leash. Then you can tell her to sit. She should know *sit* before you teach *stop.* Avoid teaching too many new commands together.

Walk a short distance, then repeat, "Stop." Repeat. Each time, your dog should be quietly rewarded for ceasing movement. In the initial learning stage, it does not matter what position your dog is in when she stops moving—it is only important that she stop moving. You can add a *sit* or *look at me for further instruction* lesson later. Do not let her become impatient or bored—many short repetitions will accomplish more than heavy-handed, ongoing repetitions. Short, frequent lessons will teach your dog, whereas prolonged boredom will teach her to break command, and result in subsequent failure for you both. With practice, she will learn that *stop* means freeze in place. Then you can begin lengthening your leash as you teach. Ultimately, your dog should become fluent enough to obey, regardless of the leash length or the distraction dead ahead.

Once your dog is fluent in *stop*, always follow a stop command with praise and a new command (e.g., *go right, go left, come*) to pull her away from danger, or give her a release word *(free dog)* when her compliance is no longer necessary. Do not let her determine when she can come off command. You must be the one to release her.

STARTING FROM A STOP

When you take the first step to begin walking, give the dog a word so she knows what is going to happen. *With me* or *walk on* are two common terms every dog can learn. Do not start walking unless you have the dog's attention so that you do not surprise and jerk her. Be polite enough to let your dog know what your intentions are. Always try to step out with the same leg—preferably the leg closest to the dog so that she has a visual cue as well as a verbal one. This is especially useful for small-statured dogs, who cannot see your face when they are at your side.

GROUND TYING

Teach your dog to *ground tie*. In the horse world, this means that when the reins are dropped on the ground in front of the horse, the horse must stay put and not walk away. There may be times when you need to leave your dog for a short period, and there is nowhere to tie her and no fence to contain her. Place your leash on the ground and tell the dog to wait. With practice, every dog can learn enough patience to hold still for brief times without wandering.

Ground tying your dogs is a clever way to temporarily free your hands.

Teach this by placing your foot or a large rock over the leash so there is tension if she does sidle away. Stand by her for a few moments, then pick up your leash quietly. Give your dog her release word and then praise her. Gradually increase your distance from her during her wait time. Do not go out of sight or far away until you are sure you dog is confident enough in your returning to not panic and pull free of the rock on her leash.

She must eventually learn that the leash on the ground is confining, even if it is not a physical hold. You are teaching a cognitive concept, which is difficult for dogs to learn. It is not a physical action like *sit* or *come*. Also, it is a psychological challenge for any dog to be left alone, even if you are just a few feet away. As your dog becomes more reliable and confident, change the order of release by quietly praising your dog when you return—before picking up the leash and freeing her. Wait a few seconds and insist she remain still as you stand near her. Then slowly bend over to pick up the leash. As you pick up the leash, give your dog your release word, and then direction for what is next, such as *walk on*.

If your dog learns to not move until her leash is firmly in your hand, it will prevent your being pulled over, especially if you are bending over tying a shoe or bagging excrement. Your commands and communication should be cheery, low key, and nonthreatening. Authoritative or loud seriousness will focus your dog's attention on your warning tone, not on learning.

KEEP YOUR DOG CLOSE WHEN APPROACHING OTHERS

When you are approaching another person face to face on a pathway, bring your dog close to your legs with an appropriate command such as *close*. Repeat if the dog needs to be brought in nearer. This will (1) keep the dog under your control and prevent tangling the leash around the oncoming person, (2) prevent your dog from jumping on the person, and (3) give the other person confidence

Avoid straight-on approaches by curving out and around.

that your dog is under your control and trained, thereby lessening any anxiety or annoyance. It is also wise to veer off the path in a curved pass to avoid having your dog fear the aggressive straight-on approach of a stranger. It also shows respect by giving the other person space. Not all people like, or feel safe, around dogs they do not know. You and your dog become ambassadors for well-trained dogs and can help another person—who has possibly had bad experiences with dogs and rude owners—to relax and enjoy the rest of their outing.

Poop Bags

Always carry poop bags and clean up after your dog, even in open spaces. Dog feces are noxious and a danger to the environment. Your dog can learn that you do this duty every time and will wait rather than pull you over.

Speak Up for Your Dog

If your dog is approached by another dog-and-person team that violates your dog's space, speak up! You must be your dog's advocate in a human world. You know your dog better than anyone, so do not allow your dog to be put upon by others' (canine or human) poor manners. If your dog is fearful, shy, or reactive, you must inform other owners that your dog does not enjoy approaches. Other owners should respect your information and keep their dog under control. If they do not, step in front of your dog, cease walking and let the others pass. Or circle wide and distract your dog with cheery chatter and tasty treats. Be careful about forcing a timid dog to turn her back on a bouncy interloper—it may increase her anxiety, which could result in fear aggression.

Greeting Other Dogs

If you wish to initiate an introduction between dogs, always ask if another person's dog is friendly with dogs (some are social with people but aggressive with dogs, and vice versa). Do not allow your dog to pull towards another dog or person without permission. If the other dog is aggressive, your naïve pup may end up hurt. Never assume that other people or dogs will welcome you or your dog.

Many dogs are fearful on walks, and you do not want to exacerbate this. If your dog is fearful or shy, be sure to let other people know. If your desire is a friendly socialization to habituate your dog to new dogs, make sure other owners know what your desires are. They know their own dog well enough to know if this will be a good encounter for your pup.

Also, for your dog's health, do not allow contact with another dog unless inoculation tags are evident. Many dog illnesses are spread through close contact, and some are airborne for long distances.

WILDLIFE

If there is wildlife in the vicinity of where you walk, keep your dog under control. Never allow your dog to chase or interact with coyotes, deer, rabbits, prairie dogs, or especially, hurt or injured animals. Bot flies/worms, fleas, ticks, and many other infectious parasites can jump or fly great distances to a host body. Check your dog after every walk to make sure she has not picked up a parasite. Other dogs that are less well attended to by their owners may be a source of contagion, as well. Teach the emergency *stop* command so that if your dog exuberantly takes off after an animal you did not see first, you can stop your dog in her tracks, before she hits the end of the leash and chokes herself or pulls you over. You should then follow up with an alternative (and hopefully higher value) command for an incompatible behavior, such as coming to you for a delicious treat instead of chasing a deer.

THINK AHEAD

Think ahead, be aware of your surroundings, and know your dog. Learn how your dog may read her situation outside the safety of her yard/territory, and be prepared to deal with her behavior by heading off problems before they have a chance to happen, seeing the world through your dog's eyes, and respecting her "dogness" by allowing her time to be just a dog for at least some of your time on each walk. Let her have time to sniff, investigate, pee, poop, and move around you. Plan dog walks for various reasons: purposeful exercise for you and her, relaxed meanderings, and/or a combination of these. Remember that safety for you, your dog, and others is of paramount importance. A walk should be a pleasant, relaxing experience for you both.

BE RESPECTFUL

Show respect for, and be polite to, all other people, dogs, wildlife, and the environment. A dog and handler with manners are welcome in all parks and public areas. Your dog will be happier with boundaries and understood rules. She will also be safer, as will others around you— animal and human.

SEVEN

CITY DOG WALKING SAFETY

Every urban dog walk should be a pleasurable time for both you and your dog, but outings do have the potential for danger. Issues may arise gradually or suddenly so you, as your dog's leader and protector, must be prepared. Go out of your way to avoid hazards whenever possible, but do know what to do if you cannot steer clear of unpleasant situations. Training is a crucial necessity for your dog's safety, because without unquestioning, immediate acquiescence to your request for attention and action, your dog may remain in a zone of danger.

HAZARDS OVERVIEW

There are many potential perils that you and your dog may encounter on even the average dog walk. These may include:

Traffic, automobiles and exhaust. Dogs' noses, sinuses and lungs are far more sensitive and vulnerable than ours. Keep away from heavy auto traffic, especially if you are running your dog and breathing deeply. Fumes are also carcinogenic.

Road Risks. Some examples are melting pavement in hot weather, broken glass and road-killed animals. Asphalt particles that are thrown up into the air by speeding tires during extreme heat can enter sinuses and lungs. If heat is severe enough to melt pavement, it will severely burn paw pad skin. Shards of sharp objects can penetrate paw pads. Corpses of decaying animals host myriad bacterial dangers—ingested or airborne.

Substrates. Some examples are hot concrete, sharp stones, burrs, and thorns. Be aware of where you are walking. Your shoes will protect you, but your dog has no footpad protection. Paw pads are vulnerable skin, filled with concentrated blood vessels and capillaries that, if infected, can pose danger to the entire body of your dog. If you must traverse such areas, use dog paw booties. Be especially careful around construction sites such as new suburban housing areas. Nails, screws, and broken glass can pose danger for unprotected paws.

Wildlife. Never allow your dog to chase or interact with wildlife, even birds. Wild animals have enough trouble surviving and do not deserve harassment. In many municipalities harassing wildlife is illegal and can result in citations and fines. Some wildlife can be dangerous, behaviorally or through disease transmission. Be especially on the lookout for snakes. Wildlife with young nearby can be aggressive, as can sick or injured animals.

Environmental Poisons. The presence of yard chemicals, by law, should be posted. Keep off and do not let the dog sniff or walk on marked areas. Many chemicals are carcinogens with dangers only known later, when it is too late.

Fast, straight-on approaches by panting runners can frighten dogs.

Pedestrians and Runners. They are frequently ignorant and may be arrogant. Do not allow them between you and your dog; avoid their straight-on/aggressive (in the eyes of your dog) approaches from the front or the rear.

Other Dogs. Whether on- or off-leash, do not allow interactions unless you know the dog is (1) inoculated and healthy, and (2) nonaggressive. When in doubt, ask the owner. Keep your distance. Protect your dog, especially if she is shy, fearful, or aggressive. Verbally reprimand the negligent owner of the off-leash dog, if necessary. If the dog is unattended, have your dog sit (a neutral body posture). Stay put until you can ascertain the temperament of the incoming dog.

Give way to speeding bicyclists by keeping your dog close and safe.

Bicyclists. They are often arrogant and dangerous to you, your dog, and themselves! Beware of their silent, speedy approaches from the front or the rear. Few follow state law and bicycle etiquette by alerting you to their approach, so it is up to you to protect your dog.

Combinations of Bicyclists, Pedestrians and Runners with Off-Leash Dogs. These ignoramuses often allow their dog to run up, around and through you and your dog, which can result in your dog becoming surprised, frightened, and then responding with fear aggression. Running off-leash dogs are vulnerable to attack and are not being protected by their person, who is ahead and speeding off. Any creature that runs (even children on bicycles) can catapult walking dogs into "prey drive"—the instinct to chase and attack. If your dog is one of the myriad breeds that manifest a high natural prey drive (especially terriers), you will have to be prepared to hold your dog back.

This scenario is a disaster in the making because it is (1) unfair to the set-upon on-leash dog; (2) dangerous for you, the pedestrian; (3) inconsiderate of a fearful dog with a history of being attacked; and (4) unkind to the loose dog that is allowed into harm's way by an unthinking and ignorant owner, who is more concerned with his own exercise than with his or her dog's, your dog's, or anyone's safety. More about safety issues and human hazards is explained in the next chapter.

AUTOMOBILE TRAFFIC

Obey all traffic/pedestrian rules and keep your dog on a short-length leash when crossing a street in heavy traffic, even in the crosswalk. Do not cross anywhere but in the crosswalk, where you are legally protected. Do not assume drivers are alert and can see your short, four-legged friend. Chances are the driver is focused on you, not something small at the end of a twenty-foot retractable leash. Do not assume drivers will give you the right of way. Be defensive, be alert and pay attention to where your dog is.

Keep your dog at your side until you are out of traffic. When walking on the sidewalk of a busy street, stay to the far side, away from the gutter, in case a car jumps the curb. Distracted drivers are every bit as dangerous as arrogant bicyclists (discussed in the next chapter). Keep your eyes open. Get away from heavy traffic as soon as possible—sensitive dog noses suffer from noxious fumes of car exhaust. Carbon dioxide exhaust can make a dog ill, especially a small dog because she is close to the ground, and on hot days when low-lying ozone is an issue.

If you must walk on concrete or asphalt on hot days, such as when crossing streets, either pick your dog up and carry her, or move quickly to a cooler substrate such as grass or soil. The longer a sensitive dog paw pad stands on a burning street or sidewalk, the more uncomfortable and possibly injurious it will be.

Never trust a driver of a thousand-pound weapon. Hit-and-run events are rampant. Personal accountability and responsibility is at an all-time social and cultural low. Protect your dog by avoiding any possible scenario that may result in the loss of your pet, as well as a lifetime of nightmares or injury for you.

WILDLIFE

It is illegal in most states to allow dogs to chase wildlife. It is also dangerous for the wild animal and for your dog. It is irresponsible and thoughtless on your part. This includes geese and other birds. More and more urban areas are being built with open areas and parks—perfect rest, feeding, and habitat-friendly areas for wild critters of all kinds. Wild animals have a tough enough time finding food, shelter and protection from natural predators—they do not need the added aggravation and danger from your untrained, naïve, domestic dog.

What lives down there? Prairie dog, fox, coyote, rabbit, or snake?

Be especially careful in winter when hidden ice over ponds can break under the weight of a dog chasing prey. In the hot summer months, various reptiles such as snakes often lie in sunny areas such as narrow trails, neighborhood rock gardens, or warm grassy areas. Your dog will scent out such a creature before you see it and may be bitten. If the snake is poisonous, you will be in for a large veterinary bill and possibly the death of your dog.

Keep your dog on-leash and teach her *leave it* (see page 79) in case she comes across a coiled snake, rotten carcass, or hidden bunny. Teaching your dog that this firm command should make her cease forward motion and return to your side for further direction. At that moment, enthusiastic praise needs be of higher value (such as a tasty treat or squeaky toy) to your dog than the danger that may have awaited her. If necessary, a quick, mild leash jerk in these situations is justified and warranted.

Mammals

Most wildlife, if given advance warning (such as the noisy approach of a dog and person), will avoid any contact with you. Jangling tags on your dog or bells on your belt will alert wildlife before you two arrive on their scene. But not all wild animals run away. Raccoons, foxes, skunks, coyotes, and deer will defend their territories, their young and themselves if confronted. Your pampered domestic pet will not fare well in these encounters.

Raccoons are nocturnal, so unless you walk your dog after dark, you may never come across one. However, they are handy climbers, so be alert, even in your own yard at night. Raccoons can be quite aggressive, especially when resource guarding—food, water, young, or territory. The can also be as large as a medium-sized dog and carry more weight, both figuratively and literally. Their front claws are enormous and sharp, and they can inflict serious injury to nosy dogs.

Foxes are primarily nocturnal but may occasionally be seen during the day, especially in the early morning or evening. They can be cute, engaging, curious, and eager to follow your dog. Or they may be "escorting" you away from a den with pups, in which case they may turn aggressive if you stumble too close to their nest. Haze them with loud yelling, arm-waving and whistles or air horns that you can carry in a fanny pack or pocket. The more fearful of humans they remain, the safer they and their families will be from conflicts with us and follow-up law enforcement action.

Skunks are also nocturnal but are easy to run into in neighborhoods during night walks. They are naturally skittish, so they will probably be long gone before your approach, but they too will protect a den and young. Keep your dog on-leash to avoid the defensive spray of a skunk—it can blind your dog at worst and, at best, make her stink for a very long time.

Some residential areas have **porcupines**, especially new housing neighborhoods in or around natural habitats. If a dog encounters this animal, the spikey spines that the porcupine wears can embed in your dog's body and mouth, which will necessitate an expensive trip to the veterinary emergency room, full anesthesia for removal, and possible infection. Again, unless directly threatened by an off-leash dog and/or unaware human near a den with young, this creature will go out of its way to avoid confrontation.

Coyotes (discussed earlier) are becoming a huge issue in even the largest urban areas. O'Hare Airport in Chicago, San Francisco's Nob Hill, Central Park in New York City, and almost all smaller towns have coyote populations. The coyote has the most expansive range of any wild predatory mammal throughout North America. Although they prefer nocturnal activity, they can be seen during daylight hours, especially during the months of pup-raising (February through May) when increased hunting demands more risk-taking. Sometimes coyotes will lure an off-leash dog away to "play" and then quickly dispatch it. Dogs are considered competition for resources and territory. If you are walking, a coyote will escort or follow you through its territory by walking parallel to or behind you, until you are out of its claimed area. Familiarize yourself with hazing techniques and use them. Keep your dog on-leash and close by.

If you take your dog on vacation with you or board her while you are gone from your home and yard, take special precautions upon your return because a coyote may have moved into your abandoned yard and taken it over as its own territory. If you let your dog out at night alone, a waiting, defensive coyote can make quick death an unavoidable consequence of your lack of accompaniment. Lights, noise, and your human presence can urge a coyote to quickly exit your yard. Smaller dogs can easily be picked up and carried away—even over a six-foot fence. Caution is the best way to avoid heartbreak.

Like coyotes, **deer** are becoming more familiar with, and habituated to, humans and dogs, with the ever-sprawling human population of towns and cities. They are usually timid but if accompanied by young, can become very aggressive. Antler injuries to dogs are numerous (far more than coyote bites) in areas where housing has provided more availability for resources and, consequently, conflicts.

Note: Contact your state wildlife division and learn how to live with the wildlife in your area.

Reptiles, Insects, and Vermin

Many dogs, and especially young and/or small-statured ones, love to chase bugs, mice, voles, rats, rabbits, squirrels, chipmunks, and snakes. Often, they will try to follow an escaping "victim" into shrubs, tunnels, or holes. Despite these natural instincts, you should never allow your dog to follow anything into any place where you cannot see her. Snake bites, bot flies (larva that embed under a dog's skin and grow undetected into large worms), fleas, spiders, ants, mosquitoes, and other insects carry diseases that you may not know your dog has been exposed to until she becomes ill or dies. A major reason to keep your dog on her leash is that you have control over what she is exposed to, and you can easily see if she encounters anything dangerous.

Birds of Prey

Just as most urban neighborhoods have raccoons, coyotes, foxes, skunks, and snakes, many also host large birds that prey on area rabbits, prairie dogs, mice, rats, smaller birds, and cats. Some of these birds will also take small dogs for food. Leashing your small dog will keep her close to you and less likely to be dive-bombed by a hawk, eagle, or owl. Both large and small birds will protect nests and territories, and their acrobatic flying attacks can be aggressive.

Small dogs that are off-leash are easy prey for large birds, which are skilled, fast hunters. **Hawks and eagles** are primarily active during daylight hours, but **owls** are nocturnal, which make them impossible to see as well as hear. Owls are the one true silent flyer—sensitive sound equipment could not pick up the sound of an owl's wing feathers when biologists studied how birds of prey attack. Even if you do hear something, a large bird will be coming in at too fast a speed for you to save your little dog. You will have no time to interfere with an airborne attack.

Note: Respect wildlife and keep your dog under control and tethered to you at all times.

Environmental Dangers

Poisons

Toxins are everywhere. Yard chemicals, automobile drainages (such as oil, gas, or antifreeze), rotting food, dead animal carcasses, ground mold, giardia in soil, common garden flowers, and certain natural flora (such as mushrooms and holly bushes) can pose health risks to the constantly curious dog.

If you are a gardener, go to the Humane Society's website (www.hsus.com) and research all toxic yard flowers and plants. They are numerous and some are quite deadly. Avoid planting any of the listed plants within easy access of your dog. Do not assume your dog will not mouth or eat plants. The toxins can build up slowly or kill quickly. Educate yourself on what to avoid, what to look for in sick dog behavior, and watch your dog everywhere you take her. Other yards may not be as safe as yours. City parks often feature beautiful gardens, but many common plants can be toxic to an uncontrolled and curious dog.

Often your dog will smell a questionable substance before you see it. Always check out anything that your dog shows high interest in, and pay attention to the ground around you. Puppies are worse than adult dogs—like human babies, anything of interest goes into their mouths, and they will eat almost anything. Dogs are motivated to eat by scent, usually not by taste. That is why dogs in shelters who become ill with the myriad forms of kennel cough congestion become anorexic. We as humans have no clue why particular smells motivate a dog to lick, bite or swallow.

The best way to protect your dog from ingesting harmful items on your walks is to teach the simple *leave it* command (see below). While she is learning, and until your dog has fully comprehended the words, your tone should be firm enough to draw her attention away from the item for the split second it will take you to redirect her to the treat in your hand; a change of direction in your walk; or happy, high-pitched verbal praise—rewarding her for looking towards you and away from the item.

How to Teach *Leave It* and *Take It*

In the formal teaching sessions needed to teach *leave it*, you should place a small but tempting piece of food two or three feet away from your dog. Sit or kneel, halfway between your dog and the food. With one arm stretched towards the dog and holding the leash taut, but not to the point of choking, place the food on the floor in front of her and tell her, "Leave it." If she lunges, hold your leash hand and arm straight. Do not allow her to grab the food. Within a few seconds, reach with your free hand and pick up the treat. Move it quickly to her mouth, and when she opens up, say, "Take it," and immediately give her the food.

Showing your dog that you will always give her the treat after a certain waiting time will teach her to trust you. Do not start with long wait times. As she becomes more patient and trusting, randomize and gradually increase the time and decrease the distance (more temptation) between leaving and taking the treats. While she is learning and developing trust in you, never tell her to leave it and then not give her the treat. Also, stay alert, and do not let her pull forward and take the treat without permission. This will teach her failure. She will have succeeded in obtaining the treat but failed in learning the lesson. If your dog is not food motivated, another item of value to her, such as a toy, will work.

Continually practice with different distances, different foods, and random waiting times to keep her interest and attention sharp. Many short sessions throughout the day will keep her desire high and keep her from becoming cognitively bored or physically satiated. Randomizing the actual food used (e.g., hot dogs vs. cheese—and always using easily swallowed food, not kibble that requires prolonged chewing) will keep her curiosity active, for she will never know what tantalizing morsel she will be rewarded with.

Once your dog seems to have a thorough understanding of both *leave it* and *take it* in whatever room you begin your lessons, travel throughout your house so her knowledge is generalized—or understood from one location to another. She must learn that the commands mean the same thing, whatever your location. Next, practice outside. Your dog should remain on a short leash until you are sure she will leave a treat untouched without permission to eat it.

Set up your dog for success by leash control.

Always provide the reward from your own hands or voice to teach trust.

When you feel confident your dog will obey the *leave it* command regardless of leash length, take her on a walk to proof her performance. Set her up by placing treats at intervals along a specific walk route, prior to taking her out. When you get close to a hidden treat, leave your leash loose with only enough slack to be able to control her if she ignores or does not yet understand your command to *leave it*. When your dog succeeds in leaving the treat when you tell her to, pick up the treat and tell her to *take it*. When she does, praise her lavishly. She must learn that edible food *only comes from your hands*.

Repeat the tests with many treats in randomized distances along a planned walk route over several days. When your dog has reliable responses to *leave it/take it*, you can utilize *leave it* on something she doesn't get. Again, plant toys or other high value items along your walk. When you tell her to *leave it* and she does, be ready to pop a handful of treats into her mouth. Large rewards are called *jackpots*. Jackpot reward every large accomplishment—and your reward treats should be more desirable and of higher value to her than whatever it is she has found on the ground.

Reinforce her learning throughout her training period by always carrying a pocketful or fanny pack of small tidbits so you can reward her when she leaves an unexpected item (such as deer feces) alone and turns to you for praise on your walks. Eventually, you will be able to phase out all food rewards (primary reinforcers) and replace them with verbal and physical praise alone (secondary reinforcers). She will then trust your judgment and leave questionable, and possibly dangerous, edibles alone on your walks when you tell her to. Always praise her when she does—never take her obedience and trust for granted.

As her fluency of the words *leave it* becomes generalized to all items and various places, you can also use the term for telling her to avoid other animals (that may be aggressive), shrubs (that may hide snakes), or any potentially hazardous scenario.

Continually reinforce *take it* whenever you give your dog anything—the word teaches her to trust that you will always "trade" with her. If you force her to give something up, you will replace it with something of equal or greater value to her. Sometimes *take it* can be just the deliverance of something wonderful—without a *leave it* involved—such as her dinner. When you gain your dog's trust in your judgment of the taking and giving of valued resources, your relationship will strengthen. But it remains crucial that she understand that all valued resources for consumption only come from your hands.

Sometimes problems do not come from "things" on your walk. Sometimes they come from other people. Insensitive, ignorant, or uneducated people can present hazards to your dog—and to you, too.

EIGHT

HUMAN HAZARDS

When you and your dog walk in a city environment, it is unavoidable that issues with people will occur. The more prepared you are, as your dog's protector and advocate, the better you will deal with questionable occurrences. What situations might you find yourself in? Who will you encounter and what circumstances may become problems? Here are the most common possibilities that you might encounter.

PEDESTRIANS

People who walk without a dog do not understand, or think about, the dynamics of walking with a dog. When a person approaches you and your dog on the same trail, curve out and away from the other person. Dogs never approach others (animals or people) in straight-on lines; they curve their approach to show politeness.

Straight-on approaches are considered aggressive by most dogs, unless they are well socialized to the peccadilloes of human behavior. Even highly socialized dogs can be frightened by speed and what can appear to them to be aggressive approaches.

Curving your approach to other people (even if you are just passing by) will often take the scariness out of meeting unfamiliar people for your dog. This will also keep the person from bending over, smiling at your dog, reaching over her head to pet, and making direct eye contact while looking at your dog's face—all of which are aggressive behaviors. If you are far enough away and curved in approach, the person who wants to interact with your dog will have to turn sideways, ask you, and will only have access to touch your dog's back or shoulder—polite and safer.

Curve around and avoid straight-on approaches,
especially with timid dogs.

A curved approach is crucial when there is more than one person coming toward you and your dog. A "pack" of unfamiliar people coming straight at her may confuse and frighten your dog. Watch her body language. If she is timid, she will lag behind you, lower her head, avoid eye contact by turning her head, lick her lips, and perhaps attempt an even wider arc than the one in which you are walking. If she is fear-aggressive, she may lunge, bark, and pull at the leash, which—though this appears to be aggressive— is often the dog's best attempt to scare off someone who scares her.

If your dog is confident and well socialized to human body language, she will eagerly look at the oncoming person, wag her tail, arch her back, and wiggle a curved-body welcome. Or she may pull toward the person, in an upright posture with her ears forward and face relaxed. If you choose to interact with pedestrians, make sure your dog is trained to not jump up, which is considered rude by people, although it is the opposite to a dog.

BICYCLISTS

These are the most dangerous and often the most arrogant and rude people you will encounter. They assume you will get out of their way, and most do not slow down or alert you if they are coming up behind you and your dog. Anything that approaches a dog from behind, especially if that approach is silent, fast and straight-on, will frighten even the most secure dog. If you walk on multiuse/bicycle trails, always look in all directions at all times, especially behind you. Never assume a bicyclist will go around or slow down. If your dog gets hit, she will be hurt. Or her frightened jump out of the way can cause you to be pulled into the oncoming biker's path and then injured.

Move over and take your dog out of confusing,
multi-stimulating scenarios.

Bicyclists are oblivious to how dangerous a speeding bike is when it suddenly stops and their body does not. Countless broken collarbones, broken arms and head injuries result from crashes on bikes. When wheels get entangled with a leash, your dog may be dragged until the bicycle stops. She can be choked, hurt, and frightened. You can be sued by the cyclist and, regardless of who is at fault, lawsuits are rampant, long, laborious, and expensive, even if you and your dog are innocent victims. More commonly, bicyclists will jump back on their bike and disappear, leaving you with an injured dog and no way to have authorities go after the negligent bicyclist.

Your dog may be left with chronic fear—of walks, of the leash, of that area, or of going outside in general. You may never know that a new behavior problem is the result of the way your dog psychologically processed a traumatic event. Dogs develop phobias easily, and one encounter with a crazy bicyclist may leave her paranoid about going out with you again.

Your own peace of mind will also suffer if your pet is injured or you are hurt. There are many obnoxious bicyclists, so avoid them in every way possible. Wear a camera, carry pepper spray and always have a phone handy, in case of bicycle road rage—which is unfortunately common.

The easiest way to avoid danger when you see an oncoming speeding bicyclist is to tell your dog to stop, sit, and wait on the side of the trail. Inexperienced or fearful dogs can be distracted with a tasty treat or squeaky toy while looking up at you. Remain still so the bicyclist has no reason to come near. Do not allow your ego and desire to hold your own space place your dog in a position of danger. If an arrogant bicyclist shouts obscenities or threatens you in any way, immediately dial 911 and give the dispatcher a full physical description. And if you have a camera recording, offer it to the police department. If the bicyclist remains or approaches you, make sure they know you have the police on the phone and are recording their verbal threats.

* * *

I once had an aggressive bicyclist yell obscenities at me (despite having three dogs with me) while I was walking in a field next to a bicycle trail (we were not even close to it). Maniacally, he yelled that a dog walker once caused him to fall and that I was "too close." He stopped, got off his bike (an expensive brand, which he threw to the ground in his fury) and was coming through the grass at me and my dogs. I immediately called 911 and got a sharp dispatcher who sent an officer to me right away. I described the man to the dispatcher, who relayed my information to the officer en route.

I filmed on my head-mounted GoPro camera and held my phone so the dispatcher could hear his ravings. He then told me he was an off-duty police officer in an attempt to intimidate me. Having been a dispatcher myself, I asked to see his identification. Since he had none, he retreated to his bike and speedily rode away. No police officer (on- or off-duty) will contact you and not show identification if you request it. Impersonating a police officer is a major crime.

I informed the dispatcher that I was headed for a clump of trees to wait for the real officer because I did not want to still be out in the open if the maniac had second thoughts and returned. She relayed my location and the real officer came to me after a search of the park around me.

Always file complaints with local law enforcement so that there is a paper trail. Anyone who manifests this type of behavior will do it to others, and it helps the police establish a record of ongoing threats and behavioral patterns.

* * *

Another day, I was walking on a pedestrian trail in a neighborhood open space. My dogs and I were the only ones in the vicinity until a young boy rode past on a speeding bicycle. As he passed me within inches, he kicked out at one of my three dogs, who was directly in front of me.

He knocked her over with the force of his kick, and then he sped straight at my little dog, who was at the end of a twenty-five-foot flexi leash, sniffing. If this delinquent had hit my little guy (who had come to me as a medical foster for a broken back and hind leg), he could have killed him. I immediately began to yell obscenities that would have burned the ears of a sailor. I carry small rocks with me, and I began throwing them. The kid swerved at the last second when a rock hit his back. Then he rode off without slowing down. I did not have my GoPro camera on that day since the weather was cold, and I thought I would be only one out.

I quickly called 911 and gave a description of the kid, his bike, his helmet and his clothes, as well as the direction of his escape—which was on a paved trail on flat ground and easy to see. The quick response by the dispatcher had a police officer waiting for the kid by the time he arrived at the far end of the trail at a street intersection. The kid was cited and his parents contacted.

Going a step farther, I posted the encounter on a multineighborhood website, and several other people (dog walkers as well as other pedestrians) responded with similar stories of the same kid's speed, aggressiveness, and dangerous rudeness. I turned all the emails over to the police, and they had an even stronger case to pursue.

Arrogantly, and oddly, the kid confronted me again a few days later—even though I had my GoPro on and was filming—as I was walking again in the open space behind our suburban home. He passed me, returned and accosted me. I ignored him—silence can be a wise response. When his tirade brought no other action from me but a stony, sunglassed stare, he eventually rode off. Again, I turned the GoPro recording over to the police, which only added to the considerable file on his behavior and resulted in more legal action for his parents.

* * *

On another occasion, I was walking my dogs near but not on a concrete bicycle/pedestrian trail when a thirty-something woman sped by on her bike. Strangely, once past me, she stopped abruptly and began yelling at me about how dogs should not be on the trail (which we were not—but the trail she was on was in my city, which I had paid for with my taxes, and which I knew to be a mixed-use trail). Once again, I remained silent, filming with my GoPro. She also dropped her bike and came at me and my three dogs. I took refuge behind a trash can as my dogs lunged and barked at her. She seemed to snap out of whatever fury fit she had been in and backed away, picked up her bike, and sped away. Everyone around us (other pedestrians and Frisbee players on the course we were next to) stood and stared in disbelief—as did I. She was never caught that day, but I have no way to know if the police were able to trace her through other disturbances.

* * *

American society is disintegrating in urban and suburban populations. Rudeness, arrogance, aggression, and "me first" attitudes abound. Do not confront or respond to anyone exhibiting aggressive mental illness. You will not win. Protect yourself and your dog with pepper spray, cameras, and silence. Contact your local law enforcement, even if the aggressor rides away. Police need immediate information, detailed descriptions, and evidence. They will open files on incidents and, even if you never hear the results, it may be that your aggressor has accosted others and is finally apprehended. You owe it to yourself, your dogs, other pedestrians, and certainly other dogs to report incidents—and find self-empowerment through action.

PEOPLE WITH OTHER DOGS

What to do if you and your dog are approached by an on-leash dog and ignorant owner

Straight-On Approaches

If someone approaches you straight-on with their dog also leashed, curve around them. As you pass, if the other person tries to engage you in conversation, explain that dogs are uncomfortable in straight-on approaches. If you approach someone with multiple leashed dogs, give them a break and curve around even wider. It is more difficult to control multiple dogs than your single one. Be considerate by giving them the right of way.

Do not "play chicken" and see which person will give way first. A dog walk is always about the dogs—yours and the other person's. If the other person appears to have a power issue, give in for all the dogs' sakes. Give way and curve around, even if you have to step onto the grass or into a gutter.

Greetings

Speak up if someone wants to allow their dog to interact with yours and you know your dog is uncomfortable. You are your dog's advocate and protector. Do not let your own insecurities (What will that person think if I don't stop to chat?) or human social requirements (eye contact, smiling and straight-on greeting) make you ignore your dog's comfort. Do not look at the other person—watch all dog body language. A change in dog attitude and greeting can occur in a split second, so you must carefully focus on the dogs, not the person.

If you want to walk with someone else (e.g., a neighbor you run into), greet the person verbally but keep your eyes on all the dogs' interactions. Watch body language and be prepared if any of the dogs appear uncomfortable. Sunglasses are great to hide where your eyes actually are looking, and you will not be considered rude to people when you are busy watching the dogs. If you wish to focus your attention on a dog, take off your sunglasses, because most dogs are insecure if they cannot see your eyes and full facial expressions.

Begin the group walk with distance between dogs. As they engage in "displacement activity" (sniffing, pooping, peeing) and grow accustomed to each other's proximity, you can walk closer to your human friend and carry on a conversation. But continue to watch the dogs. Be careful to avoid tangled leashes. If a conflict arises and the dogs are entangled, panic may result in injuries to dogs that would normally take submissive stances for appeasement but are unable to due to a knot of leashes.

Let meeting dogs determine their approach
if they appear friendly towards each other.

What to do if you and your dog
are approached by an off-leash dog

Other dog walkers can be hazardous as well. Most dogs are not well trained and not particularly bonded to their humans in an open environment. This is most evident in off-leash dogs. If there is a strong pack bond between a dog and her owner, the dog will stay close, but evidence of a weak relationship will result in a dog that runs everywhere and ignores calls. Fast, oncoming, loose dogs can frighten your dog, especially since she realizes she is restrained by a leash. The dynamics between one on-leash dog and off-leash dogs can be complicated. Dog-to-dog encounters generally go better if both are either on-leash or off-leash.

If an off-leash dog approaches you and your dog, watch the body language between the dogs, but do not tighten up your leash. This will panic your dog. She may read that you are unsure, so she will be too. Fear aggression from confinement is very real. Instead, leave your leash loose and talk cheerfully to both your dog and the other dog. Allow natural dog greetings, which will usually diffuse dog-to-dog confusion and subsequent misinterpretation of intention between the dogs.

Aggressive Loose Dogs

Ready your pepper spray in case the other dog is aggressive towards you or your dog. If the other dog is aggressive, step forward, make your body as big as you can, and be ready with your pepper spray. Your stepping forward should halt the incoming dog's approach because most dogs are afraid of larger entities coming at them. The dog may halt but continue aggressive threat displays such as barking, growling, teeth-baring and pseudo-lunging. Hold your position and remain standing still.

Try to keep your dog behind you—in a sit/stay position, if possible. The position of sit is a neutral body posture between dogs. If the dog is close and real biting appears imminent, spray the dog directly in the face. The oncoming dog should be startled at the spray and run away. If you miss and/or the dog does not run, stay calm, make yourself bigger, and do not make direct eye contact, although you should keep an eye on her movements.

If there is an owner in sight, yell at that person to get their dog on-leash or else you will spray their dog (again). When the other dog is leashed, slowly walk away. *Do not talk to the other person.* Cease all interaction and get your dog out of there. Do not respond to the other owner's excuses, and do not escalate any argument. Keep your spray handy, in case you need it for the other person. Aggressive dogs most often belong to aggressive humans.

Under all circumstances, you must keep your own emotions under control because your dog will pick up your anger or fear and transfer that to the next dog-to-dog encounter, causing her confusion and unsureness. The easiest way to control your emotions is to walk away and ignore the other person—rather than getting into a blame game and shouting match. Angry vocal assaults are exactly what you should avoid around your dog because she will have no way to know if she is the one being chastised or not. Adrenaline and loud vocal noises will frighten your dog, and she may see you as unpredictable. She has no ability to comprehend that you are focusing your anger on a stupid person and not her. If the other person responds with angry yelling and aggressive body posture, your dog (especially if she is already on the timid side) may physically feel caught in the middle, which can result in fear-aggressive lunging, barking, and biting attempts. Then both dogs may go after each other, and you will have ignorantly escalated the encounter.

Protect yourself and your dog by getting away and reporting the behavior of both the dog and person to local law enforcement. Try to memorize physical appearance details to assist the police. Give as complete a description of the person and the dog as possible. Such an irresponsible person should be ticketed and fined. They also need a lecture on protecting their own dog, which the police may or may not deliver.

Friendly Loose Dogs

If a loose dog comes towards you and your dog and shows only friendly, welcoming body posture, keep your leash loose and your voice cheery. Let the dogs interact normally until the other owner gets their dog back on-leash. Stop forward motion and wait until the owner comes forward to get their dog. If they do not come, but only stand and call their dog—and if their dog does not

Non-threatening body language by both.

respond to the recall command—tell the person to come and get their dog. Do not drag your dog away—no dog likes to be made vulnerable by being forced to turn her back to a dog she does not know. Moving away can kick the loose dog into prey drive, and that dog may chase, tease or attack your dog.

Stand still. Once the other dog is leashed by their owner, calmly explain that dogs can be frightened of new dogs and that unsupervised greetings can easily turn into fights. Be polite but firm with the other owner. Stress that although your dog is friendly and confident (if she is—if not, explain that too), others may not be, and the loose dog may be severely injured in an unsupervised encounter. Then quietly walk away and praise your dog. A quick attempt to educate an ignorant, irresponsible owner is all you should do. Do not stand around and listen to a litany of hollow excuses, especially if the person is deaf to the learning you try to impart.

If an off-leash dog is injured by an on-leash dog, the off-leash dog's owner will be ticketed and fined. But it is rare that a dog owner at fault will stick around long enough for the police to arrive. So, play it safe and do all you can to avoid conflict—for you and your dog. Keep your GoPro on, even if the other owner asks you to turn it off. Most people remain nicer if they think they are being filmed.

Note: No dog should ever be allowed off-leash unless she is 100 percent reliable with verbal and hand signals in all environments. Reliability must be proofed with instant and consistently perfect recall. If a loose dog does not immediately return to her owner when called, despite distractions, the dog is not off-leash safe. Be especially careful of allowing older, hard-of-hearing or -seeing dogs off-leash. They can easily wander into danger and not hear your recall or see your hand signal to return.

What to do if you and your dog are approached by stray dogs

If a loose dog is not accompanied by a human and approaches, stand still until she moves away. If you hold still and do not reinforce the dog through vocal or physical activity, she may go away. All dogs seek interaction, even if it is negative interaction. Watch body language between the dogs. Your dog can tell you if the newcomer is friendly or not, and if you are familiar with your own dog's body language, you will be able to see if she is comfortable.

Only when the stray leaves, should you slowly walk backward. Watch her and never turn your back—you may kick an aggressive or playful stray into prey drive. Keep your own dog close to you, and do not allow her to interact with the stray if the dog appears dominant or aggressive. If the dog returns, repeat the above behavior.

Aggressive Strays

If the stray circles and shows aggressive body posturing, call 911 and give them a detailed description of where you are and what the other dog looks like. Do not attempt to catch, tame, or interact with any dog you do not know. There are many types of aggression and unless you are a professional and know what you are seeing, do not attempt to make contact or escape. You can, however, try to calm all the dogs by humming happy, peaceful tones. If possible, keep your own dog(s) in sit position, which is a neutral body stance to most dogs. Wait until the other dog becomes bored and wanders away or until professional help arrives.

Shy Strays

The same is true of a fearful dog. If you encounter a fearful stray dog, call for professional help from your city animal control police officers. Fearful dogs can easily feel cornered by a human Good Samaritan. The transition from cowering in fear to full-blown fear aggression can be shockingly fast. Do not place your dog or yourself in a position of possible attack.

If the dog becomes attached to your dog and seems comforted by a dog companion, walk home and let the other follow, if she wants to. Alert your animal control dispatcher to what you are seeing and doing, and give them your address. If the dog enters your yard with your dog, quietly close your gate. You may take your own dog inside and let the stray loose in your yard, where at least she will be safe. Wait for animal control to arrive and take the dog. They will try to find her owner. The dog will be safe until claimed.

Note: Sometimes stray dogs who are well socialized will relax in your company. If this happens, offer treats and water. Observe the dog, and if she solicits attention in a friendly way, see if there is owner contact information on her tags. Stand to the side of the dog to remove the collar for the tags. This position will be less threatening and will keep you safer. If the dog has no collar or tags, let animal control come and take her. They have scanners to search for microchip presence and information.

ABOUT CHILDREN

Teach your children all of these lessons. In Humane Education, we teach children confronted by strange dogs to "stand like a tree." That means freezing in place, standing up straight, and not making direct eye contact with the stray dog. Above all, teach your children to never, ever run *toward* a dog and never, ever run *away from* a dog. Running toward a dog out of enthusiasm will frighten the dog due to the quick, unsolicited, and unwelcome straight-on approach, and it may result in fear aggression. Children easily panic if they become frightened and act without thinking if an unknown dog approaches them. If they run away, they can trigger the dog's prey drive, which will result in a chase—either to play or attack.

Children should tell an adult about loose dogs, and the adult should call local animal control officers. Children should never attempt to handle dogs they do not know. Children are not aware of how aggressive their normal body language is to most dogs. They are fast and loud, and even the most kindhearted child can frighten dogs that are not familiar with, and accepting of, children. Many local shelters have humane education classes available for children. Check yours and see if your child can attend these important learning opportunities.

Beware of speed, straight on, multi-stimuli hazards
with insensitive humans.

JOGGERS, RUNNERS, AND SKATEBOARDERS

This category of human hazards generally consists of boys and men, but not always. Beware of their straight-on, seemingly aggressive approaches, and be prepared to protect your dog's physical and psychological sense of safety.

Speedsters Coming from Behind

Runners and skateboarders are unbelievably stupid around dogs. They ignorantly and dangerously come up from behind a dog and owner, and 100 percent of the time, never say a word. At least some bicyclists (perhaps

10 percent) heed state law and announce they will pass "on your left." Runners almost never say anything. Their silent (due to padded running shoes, wind direction, etc.) and fast approach from behind—in most dogs' blind spots—can cause even a well-socialized and confident dog to startle. Skateboarders remain silent as well, and the unusual sound of the board wheels can frighten an inexperienced dog.

Surprised dogs can transition from peaceful sniffing of the ground to aggressive threat displays in microseconds. When a frightened dog goes into the "fight" of the "fight or flight" limbic/primitive fear response to a perceived attack, you will be jerked and may lose both your leash and your dog in less than a second. Many dogs will also fight to protect their owner in a perceived attack, but they will pay the price in a court of law if they injure the attacker. Unless there is an actual assault on you, your dog may be taken away by law enforcement and/or euthanized for aggression.

Straight-On Approaches

Other runners and skateboarders ignorantly come right at you and your dog. This fast, aggressive, straight-on approach can easily frighten your dog. Again, the dog's instinct to self-protect may kick in before you can react. Be aware that the heavy breathing of a runner mimics the threat breathing of an aggressive dog right before it attacks. Your dog will hear it as an immense threat.

* * *

Once I walked my three dogs with a friend and her dogs. We were two adult women plus six on-leash dogs, and we created a sizeable pack. At one point on our walk, we became confined by a fence around a soccer field on our left, and a row of cars parked on our right. Our dogs knew each other, and I had no fear of their having an unfriendly response to confinement. Yet had I been alone, I would have avoided this scenario. It was a short distance, and no one else was on the sidewalk we were on. I let down my guard.

Out of the blue, a woman ran right through us—dogs and walkers! Neither my friend nor I, nor any of the dogs, heard her coming. As my mouth dropped open at her ignorance and lack of awareness, along came her ten-year-old son—right through us, following in his mother's footsteps! The second startle for all six dogs was immense.

Being a professional humane educator, and having taught thousands of children for over twenty-five years about dog safety, I had to save the child from ignorance, and any future dog from possible justified aggressiveness. I hollered at the woman, questioning her desire to protect her young son from danger around a pack of dogs she did not know anything about. She stopped, but nonchalantly jogged in place, and said that she "assumed they were safe."

I responded that she must have assumed her son was not going to be hit by a car when he first crossed streets, or perhaps she allowed him to play unattended for hours in strange areas. She looked at us blankly. I tried to explain the pack mentality of dogs, the body postures and breathing threats she and the son had emanated in dog language, and how much danger she had just avoided by being lucky enough to "attack" a well-trained and socialized group of dogs. She simply shrugged and trotted away, her son straggling behind, struggling to keep up with her.

* * *

Avoid runners and skateboarders. In a dog's eyes, they are aggressive in every way. Stay off their routes by walking in the grass, a field, or anywhere with less-than-ideal terrain. Runners and skateboarders tend to stay on sidewalks, so whenever possible, walk in other areas. Always watch behind and ahead of your dog, just as with bicycles and cars.

When you see a runner or skateboarder approaching, curve out and away from their route. Talk cheerily to your dog and, especially if your dog is timid, offer distracting food or toy treats until the threat has passed.

Most people are polite and easy to walk around. If you have a polite dog and you are respectful of others, your negative encounters will be fewer. Regardless, it is best to be ready, to learn from others' experiences, and to avoid human hazards as much as you can by defensive walking. Like defensive driving, defensive walking foregoes ego and power control. You have a vulnerable creature at your side and you are her only guide through the world of human city life—a world completely unnatural to every dog.

NINE

RELISH THE DOG WALK

Walking with your canine best friend(s) will probably become the brightest spot in your day. As time passes, your communication will improve, your physical stamina will grow, and your emotional bond will prove more rewarding. You will look forward to your daily dose of endorphins (exercise hormones that produce a sense of well-being). That bouncy, enthusiastic, crazy, all-over-the-place youngster will mellow into a true partner and then, all too soon, will become a senior dog whose enthusiasm will remain but whose physical abilities will begin to wane.

Relish each day, each walk, each year that you are together. As your partner moves past you in her own dog years, adjust to her needs and follow your veterinarian's advice about exercise duration, substrates, inclines, and weather precautions. If you need to, buy sweaters, use looser harnesses, and take two shorter walks a day instead of one long one. The real point is to be together, for your daily walk is also the brightest spot of your dog's day.

FROM ROMPING YOUNGSTER TO TOTTERING OLDSTER

Even when your senior loses her sight, hearing, or ability to go far, remember that new stimuli and activities will keep her engaged—with you and the world. Try to find routes that she finds interesting, even if it is just a big circle around the block or yard. Be aware of her limitations and her mental state. Be considerate by not forcing her to go where or how she cannot enjoy her time with you. Be sensitive when you begin to see she cannot navigate steep curbs, trips for no reason, or tuckers out before you are ready to go home.

There is nothing like the love and loyalty of a dog. She deserves your consideration, awareness, and loving adjustment when walks change in nature. There is never a more important time for a safe and loving tie such as a leash when your old pup cannot see well, hear your voice, or becomes clingy and needy about having you near. Protect your oldster from wandering too far, and be ever watchful for hazards and dangers she may no longer see, hear, smell, or be unable to quickly move away from. Protect her from other dogs that may knock into her—or those she shows she wishes to avoid. You cannot know where she aches, how she fears a bump, or how painful a fall is when she loses footing or is knocked over. Keep alert to fast-moving, oncoming dangers such as speeding bicycles, weaving skateboards or distracted automobile drivers. Your responsibility to keep your senior safe should remain your top priority in congested areas.

As your dog's stamina weakens, slow down. Let her set the pace and direction, as long as it is safe for her. Find other ways to obtain your own cardiovascular workout. Create walks that cater to your dog's abilities and interests. After all, she just wants to be with you. She deserves whatever sacrifices you must make in her later years.

An oldster left at home but not lonely.

When the day comes that your devoted shadow can no longer follow you out the door, try to find other ways to exercise her body and her mind. When the time comes that your buddy cannot walk, consider a wagon, buggy, platform on wheels, or any other way to get her outdoors in fine weather for a little trip around your neighborhood. Dogs' minds often remain alert and engaged, even when their bodies no longer match their cognitive ability.

Never let your oldster see you leave without her,

especially if you have a younger dog. Be aware of her awareness of her waning ability to fill your needs. Do not purposefully abandon her alone at home when you leave with another dog. Vary your departure cues and quietly slip out the door when she is asleep. Turn on mellow music, the clothes washer and dryer, or a white-noise machine. Unless she is completely deaf, the soft tones of consistent white noise will keep her calm as you depart undetected. Keep your senior foremost in your mind and concerns. Dogs are highly intelligent and sensitive to their own aging challenges. They are not oblivious to the loss of abilities that come with older bodies. Let your dog know she is still loved, valued, and an important part of your life.

Dog walking safety and etiquette includes concern for, and manners toward, your own dog. Be a person who deserves the lifetime of devotion and love your best friend has unconditionally bestowed upon you.

The Joy of Dog Walking

Once you have found the joy, peace, and meditative remedy of dog walking, you will feel naked walking alone. If you eventually find yourself without a canine companion of your own, volunteer. Local rescues and shelters need volunteers to attend to their dog residents in myriad ways. Transfer your knowledge and experience to homeless dogs, who need exercise and some one-on-one time with a person. If you make notes on what you teach your pupils, it will assist staff and new adopters with making a quicker bond with their new dog after you have contributed your valuable time, interest, and experienced training.

You could also volunteer at a senior residence and walk dogs whose owners have slowed before their dogs have. Or help busy neighbors, traveling friends or disabled folks who have service dogs.

Adopt a new friend when your circumstances allow it and when you are emotionally and financially ready. Numerous studies have shown the health benefits when walking is a daily regimen. The benefits for you double when you have a close confidant and companion who provides unconditional attention and love. You will never forget the dog(s) you have shared those precious times with, so why not begin new memories with a homeless dog—who needs you as much as you need her?

RESOURCES

Below are resources used in writing this book. Additional information and other resources may be located online.

Grandin, Temple and Catherine Johnson. *Animals Make Us Human: Creating the Best Life for Animals*. Boston: Houghton Mifflin Harcourt, 2009. Website: www.templegrandin.com.

Santos, Henri C., Michael E. W. Varnum, and Igor Grossmann. "Global Increases in Individualism." *Psychological Science* 28, no. 9 (July 2017): 1228–39. https://doi.org/10.1177/0956797617700622.

Weber, Sunny. *Beyond Flight or Fight: A Compassionate Guide for Working with Fearful Dogs*. Denver: Pups and Purrs Press, 2015.

Morris, Desmond. *The Human Zoo: A Zoologist's Classic Study of the Urban Animal*. Kodansha America, Inc. and Random House, 1969 & 1996.

Woodhouse, Barbara. *Dog Training My Way*. Berkley Books, 1982.

Humane Society of the United States (HSUS) http://www.humanesociety.org/animals/resources/tips/plants_poisonous_to_pets.html

ACKNOWLEDGMENTS

I sincerely thank all the dogs and people who contributed to this book, including:

All my former foster dogs, who needed exercise.

All the rescue dogs who craved dissipation of their anxieties through walking.

The great author and animal handling expert, Temple Grandin, PhD, who is always supportive and a great source of knowledge.

My ever-encouraging publishing coach/project manager Polly Letofsky at My Word Publishing (www.mywordpublishing.com).

My astute and professional editor Alexandra O'Connell at Your Resident Wordsmith, www.alexoconnell.com.

My oh-so-excellent photographer Patty Howe of Patty's Pet Photography at www.pattyspetphotography.com.

My creative and always spot-on cover designer, Nick Zelinger of NZ Graphics at www.nzgraphics.com.

My perfectionist interior layout designer, Andrea Costantine at My Word Publishing.

Our city's animal control officer, Faith Wilbers, who made excellent suggestions from her unique point of view.

To Denise and Don Flournoy, and their dogs, who magnanimously modeled for the illustrations.

To Lauren Brombert, proof-reader extraordinaire at Lingua Franca Creative (www.linguafrancacreative.com).

ABOUT THE AUTHOR

Sunny Weber has over 25 years of experience in animal welfare advocacy. She is a humane educator, animal behaviorist, and trainer. She believes compelling storytelling reflects her passion for seeing the world through the eyes of the animals she works with and teaches about.

Sunny has developed educational programs regarding compassion, respect, and care of domestic and wild creatures. She writes extensively on animal issues in fiction, nonfiction, and blogs.

Sunny lives in Colorado with dogs, cats and parakeets. Their yard is a Certified Backyard Habitat for birds, squirrels, rabbits, pollinators, and any other creature with fur or feathers who wanders in.

Other books by Sunny: *Beyond Flight or Fight: A Compassionate Guide for Working with Fearful Dogs* and *The Dog at the Gate: How a Throw-Away Dog Becomes Special.*

Connect with Sunny online at
www.sunnyweber.com
sunny@sunnyweber.com
https://www.facebook.com/sunnyweberauthor/
www.linkedin.com/in/sunnyweberanimalwelfareconsult/
https://twitter.com/sunnyone24
https://www.goodreads.com/sunnyweber

Made in the USA
Columbia, SC
06 September 2021

44979559R00074